Our Family History

Our Family History

Tracing Your Ancestry

Sybilla Vere

THUNDER BAY
P · R · E · S · S
SAN DIEGO, CALIFORNIA

Acknowledgments and Picture Credits

The publisher would like to thank the following people for their assistance in the preparation of this volume: Sara Hunt, editor; Deborah Hayes, production editor; Nikki Fesak, art director; Lone Nerup Sorensen, for the index; Maureen and Keith Hunt; and the staff of numerous family-history societies and archives for comments and advice. Grateful acknowedgment is also due to the individuals and institutions listed below, for permission to reproduce photographs and illustrations on the following pages: **A.I.T., Tournai:** 84T (F437-N10); ©**Larry Angier:** 41; **Author's Collection:** 20(both), 62, 66, 69(both), 70, 82; **Christian Bracacescu & Maria Uzoni:** 86; **Collection of Jean Loussier:** 96; **Nikki Fesak:** 60, 65; **Greater London Records Office:** 85 (3674); **Idaho State Historical Society:** 13 (#60-139.17), 15 (#60-139.13); **Lane County Historical Museum:** 36, 68; **Library of Congress,** Prints & Photographs Division: 7, 26, 46, 64, 84BL, 88, 89; Rare Books Division: 90; **Local History Collection, Pikes Peak Library District:** 21, 84BR; **Mendelianum Museum Moraviae, Brno:** 13; **Museum of New Mexico:** 14 (#108329); **National Archives:** 76, 81, 83; **National Museums & Galleries on Merseyside:** 78 (SB-14051-2); **Nebraska State Historical Society—Solomon D. Butcher Collection:** 8, 32, 67, 94; **Peter Palmquist Collection:** 9,12; **Pueblo Library District:** 21, 30B, 33; ©**David Rago:** 39(both); **South Dakota State Historical Society:** 30T, 38; **Wyoming State Museum–Division of Cultural Resources:** 40

Bibliography and Sources

Carey, John, *The Faber Book of Reportage,* Faber and Faber Ltd., London, 1987.

Colwell, Stella, *Tracing Your Family History,* Hodder & Stoughton, London, 1997.

Croom, Emily Anne, *Unpuzzling Your Past,* Betterway Books, Cincinnati, 2001.

Davis, William C., *Brothers in Arms,* Salamander Books Ltd., London, 1995.

Douglass, Frederick, *Narrative of the Life of Frederick Douglass,* Dover Publications, Inc., New York, 1995.

Heath, Richard, *The Victorian Peasant,* St. Martin's Press, Inc., New York, 1989.

Hey, David, *The Oxford Guide to Family History,* Oxford University Press, Oxford & New York, 1993.

Morris, Christine M., *Tracing Your Ancestors,* Salamander Books Ltd., London, 2001.

Thunder Bay Press
An imprint of the Advantage Publishers Group
5880 Oberlin Drive, San Diego, CA 92121-4794
www.thunderbaybooks.com

All notations of errors or omissions should be addressed to Thunder Bay Press, editorial department, at the above address. All other correspondence (author inquiries, permissions) concerning the content of this book should be addressed to Saraband, The Arthouse, 752–756 Argyle Street, Glasgow G3 8UJ, Scotland; hermes@saraband.net.

ISBN 1-57145-856-5
Library of Congress Cataloging-in-Publication Data available upon request.

Printed in China
1 2 3 4 5 06 05 04 03 02

Dedication

For my first cousins: John Lees, Robert Lees, Helena Akiwumi, and Catherine Barrett.

Table of Contents

The Family History Of

INTRODUCTION

"To forget one's ancestors is to be a brook without a source, a tree without a root," warns a proverb from China, a land in which long-gone ancestors not only live on in their descendants' memories, but are punctiliously honored in formal ceremonies held within "ancestral halls" and, more informally, within the home. So powerful is ancestor reverence in Chinese culture that it is believed that neglecting one's forebears will incur their wrath and bring misfortune upon the living, while honoring them will ensure their assistance in overcoming the travails of life. Similarly, in Africa, ancestors are believed to have the power to mediate with the supreme being on behalf of their children and their children's children, so that failure to consult and honor them will have disastrous repercussions. All in all, even after their deaths,

ancestors remain a vital, influential, and integral part of the family, whether its members are living, dead, or as yet unborn.

To such cultures, whose three-dimensional view of the family is one of a seamless entity embracing past, present, and future generations, the Western practice of researching one's family history must seem baffling. And it is indeed sad that our minds are so firmly fixed on the here and now, and on the short-term future, that many of us would struggle to recall the full names of our grandparents, if we knew them at all. Ask yourself, for example, what your grandmothers' maiden names were, and then test yourself further by writing down the names of your eight great-grandparents. If you succeeded, the chances are that you already have an interest in genealogy; if you didn't, has your curiosity been piqued?

 Only a century ago, families—and the wider communities to which they belonged—were more tightly knit and more likely to participate regularly in multigenerational activities, like these villagers pictured at their annual apple harvest. Today's families are often scattered, and because many children scarcely know their extended families, they may be missing out on stories of what life was like when their parents and grandparents were growing up.

WHY RESEARCH YOUR FAMILY HISTORY?

These four sisters, pictured in Nebraska in the late nineteenth century, bear a striking resemblance to one another. It is a sad likelihood that their respective great-grandchildren, who are third cousins, are today unaware of each other's existence. Perhaps several have inherited similar family looks and characteristics, and maybe some have information about their family history that they would be happy to share with their cousins if contact were to be initiated.

Our sense of identity is fundamental to our existence, defining as it does not only how we see ourselves, but, through the face that we present to the world, how others perceive us. The quest to discover and define our identity, that elusive quality that makes each of us unique, begins at birth and encompasses a complex set of contributing factors, ranging from our behavioral characteristics and physical appearance through our strengths and weaknesses in the field of human endeavor to our given names—the labels of identity. Ultimately, however, our sense of identity is most deeply rooted in the family into which we were born. Indeed, if the family can be said to be a microcosm of human society, our family, along with our place within it, can be compared both to an anchor that holds us secure when we find ourselves buffeted on the stormy seas of life and a training ground that prepares us for our voyage into the wider world.

"No man is an Island, entire of itself; every man is a piece of the Continent, a part of the main," as the English poet and mystic John Donne wrote in 1624. The need to know where we belong, how we fit into the jigsaw puzzle or "Continent" of the human race, is a basic urge that transcends both circumstances and conditioning. Children whose mothers or fathers are permanently absent for whatever reason will often, for example, become fixated upon finding a surrogate mother or father figure, while many children who have been adopted will, at some stage in their lives—often when they themselves have children—feel compelled to seek information about their birth parents. Knowing our roots is a vital ingredient in the complex recipe that makes up our sense of identity, and the richer that ingredient, the more enriched we, in turn, will be for that knowledge.

Had you been born three or four centuries ago, it is likely that there would have been little question about where you belonged, geographically or socially, for your family

would probably have been rooted in the same locality for countless generations. In Europe, however, the development of increasingly sophisticated means of travel and widespread industrialization caused social fragmentation as people left their ancestral birthplaces in search of a better life. Religious and racial persecution also played a brutal part in the uprooting of the European family tree, while the western coast of Africa was mercilessly plundered of its people to satisfy the limitless greed of the slavetraders.

Whether or not our ancestors succeeded in their dream of building a secure future for themselves and their descendants, a sadly regrettable side-effect of the social upheavals that litter modern history is our widespread ignorance of who our more distant forebears were, let alone of their life stories. In the relay race of life, the fact that we exist at all is a validation of our ancestors' success in passing on the baton, and it seems sad that we should be ignorant of

their very existence. Indeed, it would be difficult for many of us to follow the exhortation that John Quincy Adams, the sixth president of the United States, made in his *Oration at Plymouth* in 1802: "Think of your forefathers! Think of your posterity!" because we have no idea who our forefathers were. Perhaps this is the time to rectify that ignorance and to fill in the gaps. After all, we are individual links in an unbroken familial chain that stretches back until it disappears into the mists of time and that may continue far into the future.

Uncovering the details, however mundane or dramatic, of your forebears' lives will prove a fascinating journey back in time that will reinforce your sense of belonging, of identity, and of history—and, not least, your own particular place within it. And what better gift could you give yourself, and perhaps also your children, than an awareness of your heritage, along with potentially even life-saving information?

A formal portrait of a German-American mother with her eight children. Did she add this photograph to a treasured collection brought with her from Germany? Did she pass her collection on to one of her children? If so, did one of her descendants inherit it?

PRELIMINARY NOTES

My name: ....

Date research started: ....

My birthplace: ....

My home town: ....

Why I want to research my family history: ....

....

....

....

....

....

....

....

....

....

....

....

....

....

....

Historic events our ancestors participated in:

Places our ancestors have lived in:

Particular ancestors of interest:

Achievements of our ancestors:

Family anecdotes or myths to investigate further:

I AM THE FAMILY FACE

I am the family face;
Flesh perishes, I live on,
Projecting trait and trace
Through time to times anon,
And leaping from place to place
Over oblivion.
　　　—Thomas Hardy, "Heredity" (1917)

Whether or not you subscribe to the African and Asian belief that your ancestors have a direct influence on the course of your life's path, in one respect we know they do: the genetic inheritance that they bequeathed to you determines to a large extent how you look, how you behave, and how healthy, as well as how long, your life is likely to be.

When the English writer Thomas Hardy wrote the poem "Heredity" in 1917, his emphasis was on family features and quirks of behavior, but as a result of the recent strides made in genetic research, the specific hereditary gene that may literally make or break a family by compromising its members' physical or psychological health can now be identified. Perhaps the most famous family to be blighted by a hereditary genetic defect was the brood mothered by Queen Victoria, a carrier of the gene that manifested itself in the hemophilia suffered by many of her descendants, including her great-grandson, Czarevitch Alexis of Russia, who was murdered with his family in the wake of the Russian Revolution. (Indeed, some historians believe that the boy's illness was a direct cause of the revolution, the populace having been enraged by the influence that the Siberian mystic Grigori Rasputin wielded over the czar and czarina, who believed he had the power to cure their son.) Huntingdon's disease is another such serious hereditary condition, as is Marfan's syndrome, a disorder of the connective tissue. In fact, it is speculated that Abraham Lincoln, the sixteenth president of the United States, was afflicted by the latter, because his abnormal height and slenderness are hallmarks of the disease.

Each person's DNA is unique, with the exception of identical twins, who share the same genetic blueprint and therefore look alike, as well as sharing many other characteristics that their genetic inheritance has bequeathed to them.

Today, many people are being propelled into family-history research for the critical purpose of safeguarding the health and lives of future generations. Their quest focuses both on tracing the line of descent of a suspect gene or chromosome and locating long-lost relatives for genetic information. Although there is no cure for many hereditary diseases as yet, modern technology can identify the faulty genes responsible. Genetic screening can thus give prospective parents vital knowledge about any genetic aberrations that they may be at risk of carrying—but, admittedly, this results in some heart-wrenching choices as well.

For most people, however, their genetic inheritance may be nothing more sinister than the "family nose," or an innate artistic talent, and in such cases it can be fascinating to trace the aforesaid nose down the generations by studying family photographs, or to appreciate the creativity of artistic forebears in artifacts that have been passed down as heirlooms.

The children pictured with their parents above have each inherited a unique combination of the genes of both parents. The boy at right resembles his mother, while the brother sitting next to the basket looks more like his father.

Gregor Mendel (1822–84), who conducted experiments in the gardens of a monastery in Brünn, Austria (now Brno, in the Czech Republic), is known as the "father of genetics" for his groundbreaking research on heredity.

☞ *This collection commemorates an episode in the life of Clara Blinn, who was taken captive by Native Americans in 1868. Her photograph and a letter written in her hand are pictured here with a newspaper article, in which the journalist argued that her capture justified the harsh actions of the U.S. Army against the Plains peoples at that time. Discovering evidence of your ancestors' experiences brings historical events into vivid focus.*

BRINGING THE PAST TO LIFE

History is not simply a litany of dull facts contained in the pages of dusty books, but a series of snapshots of our world as it developed. And family history, in particular, is like a library of gripping novels that weave fascinating stories about the lives and times, the loves, loathings, strengths, and travails of the men and women whose blood flows through your veins—people who would not have wished to be considered irrelevant to the lives of their descendants. Put yourself in their position—wouldn't you feel disgruntled, too? One of the keys to bringing the past to life is understanding, and empathizing with, the real human concerns, problems, and aspirations of individuals who faced the future's uncharted territory every day of their lives, as we do. When you were a child, you probably found it impossible to imagine your grandparents ever having been young, just as it may be difficult for you now to equate a stiff, unsmiling figure in a sepia-toned photograph with a vivacious individual of unique personality. Yet it takes only a sprinkling of facts and a dash of imagination to transport you back to the heady days when your grandparents were setting out on life's journey together, or for that forbidding figure to step out of the confines of his sepia setting into a bustling world full of energy, interest, and color, upon which he would make his own unique impact.

Although, like us, our ancestors were primarily focused on the business of living, the wider world sometimes intruded on their daily round of work and domesticity, occasionally disrupting their lives irrevocably and thus permanently altering the nature of their families. In a letter home, Private Andrew K. Rose, of the Ohio Infantry, reported the death of just one victim of the Civil War: "Christopher Dimick was ded [sic] that makes 3 of the Dover boys that has died out of 42 and one killed. That is about the way there is more dies by sickness than gets killed." Both this civil war and the terrible global conflicts of the twentieth century wrought innumerable family tragedies by eradicating millions of brothers, sons, fathers, and fathers-to-be. Nor was war the sole source of family devastation. The Irish potato famine of 1845, for instance, condemned 1 million people to die of starvation and forced another 1.5 million to abandon their homeland, many of them crossing the Atlantic in search of a promising new start in the United States. In *A Journal of a Visit to Skibberdeen and its Neighbourhood* (1847), a first-hand account of the human devastation wreaked by the famine, Elihu Burritt described the misery that he encountered: "In one [hovel] which was scarcely seven feet square, we found five persons prostrate, apparently near their end. A girl about sixteen, in the very picture of despair, was the only one left who could administer any relief; and all she could do was bring water in a broken pitcher to slake their parched lips." Did that girl survive? Did she find a better life in the New World? Did she have children? Could she have been your ancestor?

Even in less catastrophic times, what was it like to be a seventeenth-century European countrywoman, who, along with the drudgery of her domestic and farming duties, spent most of her adult years producing children, only to lose an average three in five of her offspring before they reached their first birthday, often to a disease that can now be prevented by a simple vaccination program? Nor had the rural woman's position improved by the late nineteenth century, as the English social commentator Richard Heath recorded in 1872, following a visit to the English county of Oxfordshire:

Or you enter a cottage, and as the woman talks with you she holds her hand to her side. She has a heart complaint. And yet she has been regularly in the fields, bringing up a family at the same time, working sometimes as much as fourteen hours on a stretch. ...You ask her about the children. It is a common tale, the natural result—she has lost four out of seven.

Could factory work have been any better? Were there occasions for celebration, too? What must it have been like to live in such times? Perhaps there is a fading letter tucked away in a box of family keepsakes that will tell you.

Every baby's arrival in the world is accompanied by his or her parents' hope that their child's life will be blessed with health, happiness, and security, blessings that their respective parents once wished for them, and that the infant may one day in turn hope for his or her own children. Researching your family history will enable you to discover how your forebears fared in life.

Use this space for a
map of an ancestor's
home locality

INTRODUCTION

Use this space for a
photograph of an ancestor's
home, workplace,
or place of birth

Use this space for a copy of
a newspaper clipping or
photograph of an event
your ancestor witnessed

Use this space for a
copy of a letter or journal
entry written by an ancestor

A LIFELONG INTEREST

Over the past few decades, family history has become one of the fastest-growing of all leisure pursuits, and in response to its phenomenal surge in popularity, source material is increasingly being made available by organizations who hold relevant records. And with the flood of information on births, baptisms, marriages, deaths, burials, emigration and immigration, censuses, and military service from archives the world over being released on microfiches, CD-ROMs, and the Internet, researching your family history from the comfort of your home has never been easier.

One of the wonders of family history is that its material is virtually infinite. Although, for simplicity's sake, it's best to concentrate on one of the lines of descent that you've inherited—either your mother's or father's—when you set out to discover your roots, there are many other trails to follow if you reach an impasse. Unless any of them were cousins, in your four grandparents you have four family lines to trace, eight in your great-grandparents, and sixteen in your great-great-grandparents, the numbers doubling as you work back through each generation. Dip your toe into genealogical waters, and it won't be long before you start to identify with English writer Dodie Smith's description of family, "that dear octopus from whose tentacles we never quite escape." (*Dear Octopus,* 1938.)

The tentacles spread far and wide, and you may even discover more than you anticipated as you find yourself making contact with cousins of various degrees in different parts of the globe. This often happens when you join a local or specialized family-history society, or enter the family name into an Internet search engine. As a family historian, you are never alone: besides reinforcing your links with predecessors, you will no doubt forge new bonds with the living representatives of your bloodline, thereby reviving family ties, as well as making new friends in the process.

On a more practical note, another advantage of family-history research is that you can set it aside when real life intrudes and take it up again when you have the time to continue building on the information that you've collected. It somehow seems fitting that the study of your ancestors' lives can

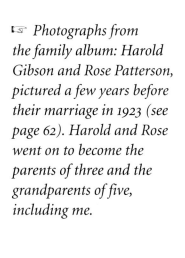

☞ *Photographs from the family album: Harold Gibson and Rose Patterson, pictured a few years before their marriage in 1923 (see page 62). Harold and Rose went on to become the parents of three and the grandparents of five, including me.*

The faces in these photographs reveal little about the personalities behind them, but by following up clues in your family history, you will learn more about the lives of those whose portraits you have inherited—that is, if you can identify the subjects in the first place!

truly be a lifelong pursuit, as well as a highly addictive and satisfying hobby. Not only will you derive great gratification from solving generations-old mysteries through your own detective work: by reclaiming your long-lost heritage, you'll gain a new appreciation of your roots, deepen your knowledge of the minutiae of the past, learn to respect your forebears as individuals, and pass on the priceless gift of knowledge to those who will carry the family name into the future.

In *The Devil's Dictionary*, the American writer Ambrose Bierce defined genealogy as "An account of one's descent from a man who did not particularly care to trace his own." Although there is a ring of truth to this tongue-in-cheek definition, it could equally be argued that the man in question had no need to trace his line of descent because it was already known to him. Nevertheless, nearly everyone who embarks on the task of compiling his or her family history will at some stage be vexed that family members seemed so lax when it came to recording, or preserving, the basic details of their lives. I, for example, was thrilled to be given a handsome album filled with photographs of people dressed in the fashions

of the late nineteenth century, inscribed to show that it was a gift from my great-great-grandfather to his daughter, Elizabeth Vere, my great-grandmother, on the occasion of her twenty-fourth birthday, January 16, 1885. Unfortunately, not a single photograph is accompanied by an identifying label, leaving me and my two new-found "Vere cousins" in England and Australia in the frustrating position of knowing that many—if not all—of these people are related to us, but not who they are (although, because family historians rarely throw in the towel, at least not yet).

Outweighing such inevitable, though often only temporary, dead ends are the "Eureka!" moments that come when you find that elusive great-great-grandmother's name in a historical record, or receive an e-mail out of the blue from someone who shares an ancestor with you, thus slotting another piece into the family puzzle. There is a wealth of information awaiting your discovery if only you know who to ask and where to look, information that I hope this guide will help you to uncover and, in so doing, bring many of your ancestors into the flow of your own life.

Overleaf ☞ Use the spaces in the following pages for photographs of relatives from different branches of your family tree.

Use this space for a
photograph of members
of your mother's family

Use this space for a
photograph of members
of your father's family

Use this space for a
photograph of your
siblings or cousins

Use this space for a
photograph of yourself
with your own family

RAIDING YOUR FAMILY ARCHIVES

You are the starting point for your research into your family history, as well as the end of the trail that will lead you back in time, so before dispatching barrages of inquiries in all directions, turn your attention to the facts that you already know. First draw up a rough family tree (see Chapter 2 for guidance), with your full name and your date and place of birth at the bottom or side, depending on your preferred format. Then extend your tree upward or sideways to include first your parents and then your grandparents, recording as much vital information as you can, such as when and where they were born, married, and, if applicable, died. If you can continue working back through the generations, so much the better.

From this first step, you can see at a glance the gaps that need to be plugged. Keep this rough tree to refer to in the future; if you've decided to focus on only one part of your family for now, it will act as a reminder of the others that are waiting to be researched; it may also prove a source of later amusement when you see how little you had to build on and how far you've come since you recorded those sketchy details. You may have been tempted to embellish the branches of your first family tree with additional twigs representing your own children, siblings, aunts, uncles, and cousins, but if your family is a large one, you may initially find such a guide too cluttered to work with (see the comparison illustrations overleaf). If the urge to document all of your known relatives is overwhelming, however, give in to it. Such information should definitely be recorded, but in the interests of clarity, it's advisable to do so on separate trees, one devoted to your mother's family; another to your father's family; and one for each of their parents' families, in which you can include siblings, cousins, and children as appropriate.

Now ask yourself if there is any material in your head or home that will flesh out the bare bones of your family "skeleton." Using separate pieces of paper headed with the names of each of the individuals on your family tree, write down anything that you know, or can remember, about their lives, such as where they lived, what they looked like, and their religion and profession, along with any anecdotes that you can recall being told about them or your personal reminiscences of them. Having plundered your memory, now scout around your home. Do you have any official documents, letters, photographs, or artifacts relating to those people that may throw further light on aspects of their lives and times? Have a root around, set aside anything that looks potentially useful, and record any relevant snippets of information on the biographical sheet of the person in question.

Having started with next to nothing, you'll probably now have at least a few names and dates to focus on. But before stepping out on the path that will lead you further into the past, take a little time to think about why you want to research your family history and also to define your objectives. Remember that your grandparents represent four different families; do you want to research them all or instead concentrate on the one that interests you the most? It will certainly be less confusing to focus your time and attention on only one family line at a time, but can you bear to ignore the other three (for the moment, at least)? Is there a family legend or mystery that has always intrigued you, and would you like to discover the truth of the tale? Think about whether one line of descent would be simpler to trace than another, too: if you know that your father's family, for example, was rooted in one place, especially if it is your own locality, it may be more fruitful to investigate that branch of your bloodline than the one

Its monetary worth may be negligible, but this piece of family memorabilia is priceless to those whose forebears have preserved it over the course of successive generations. During the mid-nineteenth century, many families endured almost unimaginable hardships as they followed the tough trail westward. Some used the canvas from their wagons as temporary shelter when they reached their destinations.

& As these contrasting examples clearly demonstrate, trying to cram all of your known relatives into one tree (opposite) will paint a confusing picture. It's therefore best to draw up separate family trees, one tracing your direct line of descent (below), and others charting the genealogical course of each of the families from which you are descended.

Jeremiah Hamilton

b. 1883, Preston, England
m. ?
d. 1916, Somme, France

James Hamilton

b. 5 Mar, 1910, Preston, England
m. 14 Jul, 1932, Carlisle, England
d. 30 Nov, 1982, Preston, England

Daisy May Carter

b. ?
m. ?
d. 1941, Preston, England

John Keith Hamilton

b. 15 Jan, 1935, Preston, England
m. 10 Jun, 1957 Hartford, CT

John Bell

b. 1891, Carlisle, England
m. 12 Apr, 1910, Carlisle, England
d. ?

Angela Bell

b. 10 Aug, 1912, Carlisle, England
m. 14 Jul, 1932, Carlisle, England
d. 26 Jan, 1984, Preston, England

Marion Fox

b. ?
m. 12 Apr, 1910, Carlisle, England
d. 1952, Carlisle, England

Margaret Judith Hamilton

b. 30 Sept, 1962, Hartford, CT

Edward Constable

b. 1881
m. ?
d. 1939, Burnley, England

Alfred Constable

b. 20 Feb, 1905, Burnley, England
m. 5 Aug, 1933, Burnley, England
d. 11 Sept, 1965, Burnley, England

?

b. ?
m. ?
d. ?

Susan Mary Constable

b. 14 Oct, 1938, Hartford, CT
m. 10 Jun, 1957 Hartford, CT

George Lancaster

b. 1881
m. ?
d. ?

Emily Lancaster

b. 25 Jul, 1908, Burnley, England
m. 5 Aug, 1933, Burnley, England
d. 2 Dec, 1974, Lancaster, England

Lucy Hartley

b. 1887, Burnley, England
m. ?
d. ?

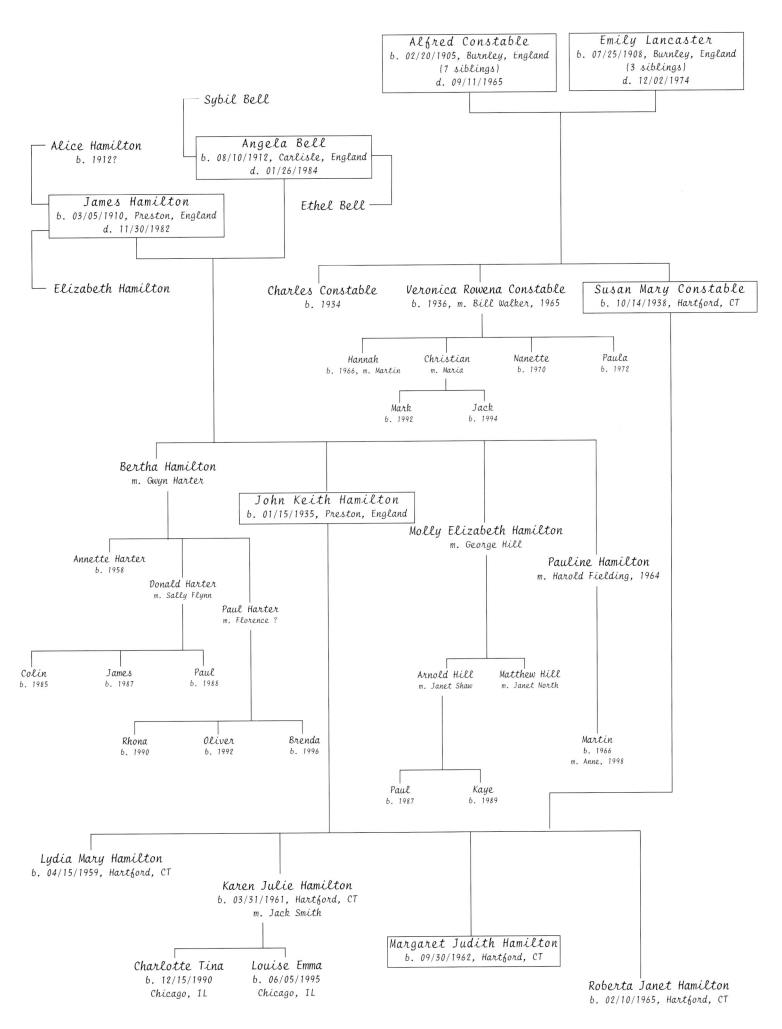

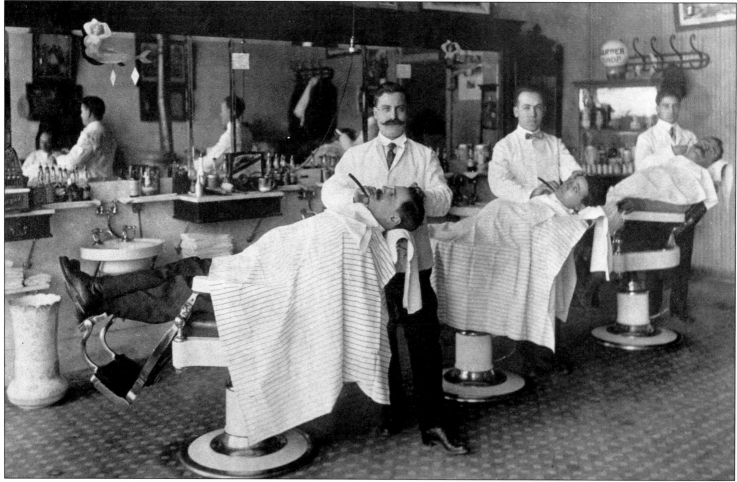

bequeathed to you by your mother, whose family may have emigrated from a country whose language you are unfamiliar with and whose archives are difficult for you to gain access to. Another consideration to ponder is whether one family has more living representatives—particularly older ones—to help you on your way than another. And has anyone already attempted to delve into the history of your mutual family? If so, will their work be a welcome foundation on which to build your own researches or would you prefer to start from scratch?

Once you begin your detective work, you'll realize how helpful this simple exercise in clarification can be in keeping your attention focused on your ultimate aim, for as you start to uncover material, you'll be presented with numerous distracting red herrings, as well as nuggets of pure genealogical gold. It's now time to cast your net wider and to ask your relatives, some of whom may possess a mine of information, if they can add anything further to your embryonic family tree. Before doing so, marshal your facts, make a list of the questions to which you'd like answers, and, finally, decide which of your relations to approach for help (see below). Although you will certainly be able to research your family history without their assistance, any information that they can give you will be a time-saving and enlightening bonus, albeit one colored by personal perceptions and experience, as well as the inevitable tricks that memory plays, so keep an open mind and don't take everything that you're told as the gospel truth (especially vague claims regarding ancestors that were royal, noble, or merely fabulously rich!) Indeed, your guiding principle should be to double-, if not triple- or quadruple-check as many of the facts that you uncover about your forebears as you can, even if they come from official sources (after all, neither clerks nor official transcribers are immune from the occasional bad day at work).

Family photographs provide a rare and vivid glimpse of your ancestors' lives and times. Perhaps your great-grandmother was the South Dakota schoolmarm who is pictured with her charges in 1897 (above), or the obedient-looking girl at right. The photograph below was obviously taken to promote this Colorado barber shop, but who are the barbers? Maybe an older member of your family can help you to identify them.

FAMILY MEMBERS TO APPROACH FOR HELP

NAME	NOTES, COMMENTS, OR QUESTIONS

PREPARING TO GATHER INFORMATION FROM RELATIVES

Sensitivity, consideration, and respect are essential prerequisites for successfully garnering information from members of your family. Although you may be fired up by your enthusiasm to discover more about your ancestry, it's important to remember that not only may your relatives remain unmoved by your burning curiosity, but that you are asking them to give up their precious time, when time may already be in short supply, to do something that doesn't much interest them. In addition, if you've persuaded a family member to retrieve the details of a distant or estranged relation from an old address book, some such recipients of a letter of inquiry may have mixed feelings about having been contacted in the first place, let alone being asked to help someone who may, after all, be a total stranger. Bear in mind that you are asking for a considerable favor and that your kith and kin are not obliged to assist you in a quest that they may consider irrelevant to their lives or that they may even feel uncomfortable with.

Older family members in particular may be reluctant to revisit memories that they perhaps find painful to recall, or maybe there's a family skeleton that they'd rather you didn't uncover, perhaps an illegitimate birth. "Accidents will occur in the best-regulated families," as Mr. Micawber, a character in English writer Charles Dickens's novel *David Copperfield* (1850) commented, and most families can point to at least one such "accident" somewhere along their line of descent. Although there is no social stigma attached to a child being born out of wedlock today, only a generation or two ago the consensus was that illegitimacy within the family was something to be ashamed of, and ingrained attitudes may die hard among the more senior members of your family. Similarly, divorce, mental illness, suicide, wild, or even criminal, behavior often fall into the category of subjects that many people feel are best swept under the family rug. Although most family historians are excited to discover such instances of difference from the social norm—human flaws and foibles somehow make a long-dead forebear more interesting—be warned that your relations may prefer not to discuss any of the family's

☞ *Harvey Andrews, his wife, and three young children are captured on camera at the graveside of a fourth child, Willie, who died at nineteen months of age. Sad images like this are often the only surviving evidence of the existence of a child who died in infancy.*

Not only do wedding photographs give you a fascinating taste of the fashion of the age, but because the siblings of the happy couple often feature in such group portraits, they can help you to put faces to many family names. If an old photograph is unlabeled, ask your older relatives if they can identify the subjects and hazard a guess at the date.

black sheep, and try to respect their feelings if they decline an invitation to share all with you. While being given a headstart in the information stakes will certainly save you time and trouble, don't become too frustrated if you find yourself being stonewalled by a recalcitrant potential source, because you'll probably be able to reconstruct sensitive family events through your own efforts.

Some of your relations may be so excited about being consulted, on the other hand, that you find that you've opened a floodgate of memories and are in danger of becoming overwhelmed by a deluge of indiscriminate facts, speculation, and reminiscences. It is therefore advisable to compile a questionnaire, a list of specific questions to which you'd welcome answers, before approaching family members, both to keep your mind focused on the primary issues and to prompt someone whose mind has wandered off at an unhelpful tangent to return to the point in question. The sample questionnaire provided overleaf includes the most useful questions you might want to ask your relatives.

Answers to questions like those on the sample questionnaire make good pegs on which to hang the details of your forebears' lives, but feel free to rephrase, adapt, or add to them in any way that better matches your family circumstances or the line of inquiry that you have chosen to follow. Once you've settled on a template list of questions that you want answers to, decide which of your relatives to target, make a copy for each of them, and write their name and the date at the top of the questionnaire for future reference.

Before distributing the questionnaires, it would be courteous to contact your potential questionees (family gatherings at holidays like Thanksgiving present the ideal opportunity for multiple targeting) to explain that you are researching your mutual family history, to ask them if they would be prepared to give you a little help, and to offer to share your findings with them in return. If they agree, you have two alternatives: first, perhaps if they live a long way away or are too busy to meet with you, you could send them their questionnaires

FAMILY QUESTIONNAIRE

DATE

What is your full name (maiden name if appropriate)? ....

Were you named for another family member? ....

Where and when were you born? ....

What is your religion? ....

Were you born into this religion? ....

Where did you live when you were growing up? ....

Where did you go to school? ....

Do you have a profession? If so, what is it and where do, or did, you work? ....

Are you married with children? If so, when and where did you marry and what are the names, dates, and places of birth of:

1) Your spouse ....

2) Your children? ....

Do you have any brothers and sisters? .... If so, what are their names, dates, and places of birth? ....

Did any of your siblings marry? .... If so, to whom? ....

Did they have any children? .... Please give their names, dates, and places of birth. ....

Do you have any photographs, documents, or heirlooms from your childhood or passed down from your parents?

PART B: YOUR MOTHER'S FAMILY

Your mother's full name, including her maiden name, and date and place of birth: ....

What was her religion? Was she born into it? ....

Did she have any brothers or sisters? If so, can you remember their names and where, and roughly when, they were born?

....

....

Where did she live when she was growing up? ....

Did she have a profession? If so, what was it? ....

What were your mother's parents' names? Do you know roughly when and where they were born? And when and where they died and were buried? What was their religion? ....

....

Did either have them have a profession? If so, what? ....

Did your mother's father serve in the military and did he see action? If so, which branch of the armed forces was he in, and where did the action take place? ....

Is there anything else that you can remember, or would like to tell me, about this family? ....

....

....

PART C: YOUR FATHER'S FAMILY

Your father's full name and date and place of birth: ....

What was his religion? Was he born into it? ....

Did he have any brothers or sisters? If so, can you remember their names and where, and roughly when, they were born?

....

....

Where did he live when he was growing up? ....

Did he have a profession? If so, what was it? ....

Did he serve in the military and did he see action? If so, which branch of the armed forces was he in, and where did the action take place? ....

What were your father's parents' names? Do you know roughly when and where they were born? And when and where they died and were buried? What was their religion? ....

....

Did either of them have a profession? If so, what? ....

Did your father's father serve in the military and did he see action? If so, which branch of the armed forces was he in, and where did the action take place? ....

Is there anything else that you can remember, or would like to tell me, about this family? ....

....

....

to fill in at their leisure. A potential problem with this approach, however, is that the completed questionnaire may not be returned as quickly as you'd hoped—if at all—in which case, allow a reasonable period of time before sending a follow-up letter of inquiry and encouragement. Secondly, you could arrange to visit them and to work through the questionnaire together, a good strategy if they live in your locality, have difficulty writing, or, you suspect, may need some gentle prompting.

It is crucial to visit very senior members of your family as soon as you can. It's a sad fact that many precious memories go to the grave with those who possess them, and time may be of the essence if you are to benefit from the richness of those recollections of generations and times past. Encouraging your seniors to share with you their memories of their parents, grandparents, and of their own lives and times, may well require time and patience, but while teasing out information may be a slow process, you'll probably both enjoy the mutual contact and company as you talk about your shared family heritage and their life experiences (some of which may astonish you). Take a notebook with you in which to jot down information and also make a note of the date of your interview and your companion's name and address (although some of the things that you are told may not

seem relevant now, they could later provide vital clues, so make sure that you preserve this record in your family archive). Another option is to make an audio or video recording of your interviewee (and if you do this, remember to label it with the subject's name and the date of the interview), which makes a more personalized and interesting record, but be warned that being recorded makes many people feel uncomfortable or inhibited about speaking or behaving naturally, so much so that they may clam up completely. They may, however, at least consent to having their photograph taken, so go equipped with a camera and, at the end of your visit, ask if they'd mind you taking a snapshot of them for the family album. Use the space opposite to display a photograph of a family member or family group.

The result of your initial foray into your family's collective memory will, with luck, have produced a flurry of papers filled with names, dates, places, and reminiscences for you to process. Remember, however, that memory can be faulty and that you should therefore check as many pieces of information as you can against official documents, such as birth certificates, for accuracy. Now you have something to work with, but before starting to collate your data, try to find out whether a member of your family has any more tangible records of your family history.

☞ *In the days before television introduced the couch-potato phenomenon, families made their own entertainment. A photograph like this may prompt senior members of your family to share interesting memories about what life was like when they were growing up.*

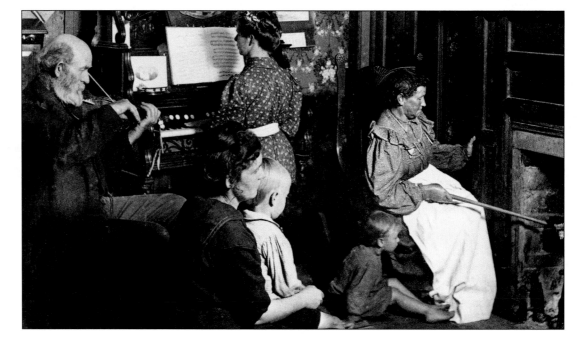

Use this space for a copy
of a family photograph
provided by a relative

☞☞ *While a century-old diary (above) may provide you with the minutiae of a forebear's daily life, antique furniture and textiles (below) can tell you much about the taste—and financial means—of their original owners.*

During the Victorian and Edwardian eras, ladies indulged their passion for filling scrapbooks with photographs, poems, pressed flowers, or sketches. Ask your relations if they have inherited any such keepsakes—they may provide an illuminating insight into their compilers' lives.

HAND-ME-DOWNS AND HEIRLOOMS

You and your fellow family members may be harboring a treasury of vital aids to your research in your homes. Anything that has been handed down through the generations, be it jewelry, furniture, a patchwork quilt or handstitched sampler, a gallery of faded photographs, a cache of letters or other types of written documentation, could yield valuable clues about their original owners. Many sentimental keepsakes will have been distributed among siblings either during their parents' lifetimes or after their deaths, while vital records, such as birth, marriage, or death certificates, along with heirlooms of particular significance to the family—perhaps wedding rings or pocket watches—will often have ended up in the safekeeping of eldest children or their own heirs.

To obtain details of any surviving family hand-me-downs and heirlooms, you'll again have to depend on the goodwill and willingness of your long-suffering relations to scour their homes to bring them to light. Ideally, you should examine any family artifacts or paperwork yourself, but if this isn't possible, ask the owner(s) at least to write out a detailed description of their items and perhaps, especially in the case of jewelry, medals, or furniture, to photograph them (which is in any case advisable for insurance purposes) and to give you a copy for your family archive. Ask them to make a note of anything that they remember about an article's provenance, too, such as how it came into the family, to whom it originally belonged, and to whom it later passed, so that you can link it with named individuals and thus maximize its clue-giving potential. If the heirlooms in question are letters, diaries, official documents, family photographs, birthday books, autograph albums, or newspaper cuttings, ask for photocopies (and advise them that because old pieces of paper may be fragile, the photocopying process should be carried out with care), and offer to reimburse the copying cost or make the copies yourself. Failing that, in the case of written documentation, beg your relations to jot down as much of their vital data as possible. If anything is loaned to you, be sure to treat it with kid gloves while it's in your possession and restore it to its owner as soon as you are able.

If your relatives are cooperative, you may find yourself rejoicing in a wealth of information. Not only can full names, dates, and place names be found in vital-record certificates, but a newspaper cutting—which must, after all, have had some significance for someone to have thought it worth preserving—may report a family triumph or tragedy and pinpoint your ancestors to a specific place, while a yellowing letter may tell of a soldier's harrowing experiences at the front or of a daughter's first taste of married life. An old wedding ring may be engraved with the initials of the bride and

groom, along with the date on which they were joined in matrimony—and perhaps a sepia-toned photograph portrays the happy event—while an inscription on a pocket watch may reveal that it was a coming-of-age gift from your great-grandparents to their son. A sampler may be stitched with the name of its creator and the date of its completion, or a patchwork quilt spell out a family tale in its geometrical symbols. That dusty book that no one's ever really looked at before may reveal on its flyleaf that it was a prize presented to your ten-year-old grandmother by her school as a reward for excelling at arithmetic, and if you are very lucky, a family Bible may even list the full names and dates of birth of its original owner's children.

As well as yielding potentially helpful information to speed you on your way, such items are touching testimonies that reveal glimpses of the personalities of your fore-

bears and the things that they held dear. They represent a precious part of your family legacy that should be handed down to the next generation intact, so respect and cherish them while they are in your care.

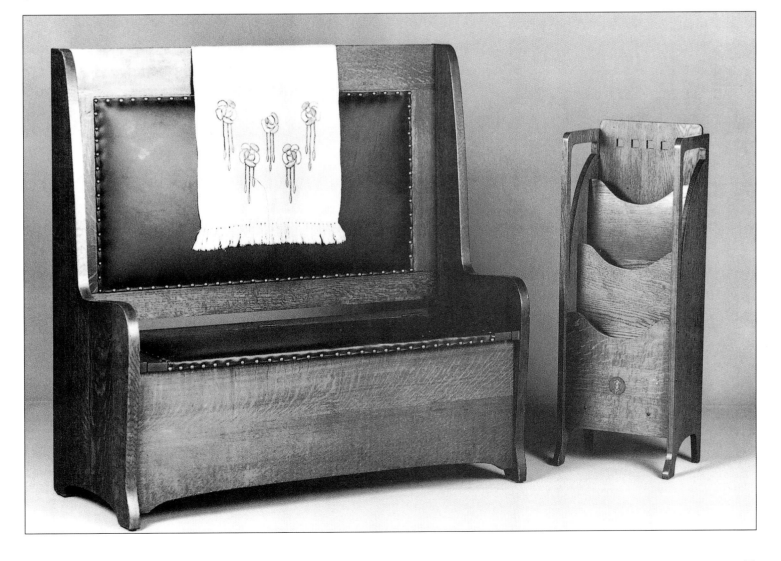

A MESSAGE FROM THE GRAVE

A final preliminary avenue that may prove fruitful (and fascinating) is that melancholy road that leads to the grave. Memorial inscriptions on tombstones will usually furnish you with a forebear's name, date of birth, and date of death, and possibly also the names of that person's parents, spouse, or children (whose existence may otherwise be difficult to discover or establish if they died in infancy). Such vital information is occasionally accompanied by an epitaph—either personal or drawn from religious scriptures—that will give you a flavor of your forebear's character or, perhaps more pertinently, how the bereaved wished their loved one to be remembered for posterity.

Whether by accident or design, the deceased members of many families, especially those that have lived in the same locality for generations, are often buried in close proximity to one another, either in the same plot or in neighboring graves, thereby enabling you to record a wealth of detail relating to several people in a single visit. The location of the family graveyard may already be familiar to you, but if it is not, before setting out to visit a promising cemetery (or, if its location is prohibitively distant, asking someone who lives locally to track down memorial information for you), it's advisable try to ascertain that this is indeed the likely final resting place of your family member or members. Do this either by questioning your relations or by contacting the authority responsible for the burial ground's running and maintenance to ask if it would be willing to check its records to establish whether they contain any matching names. Alternative sources of information that can help you to pinpoint who is buried where include local family-history societies, many of which run recording programs staffed by volunteers, as well as a number of specialist websites, such as those listing the names and burial sites of soldiers who fell in foreign fields while fighting for their country.

It is a strange feeling when you finally find yourself gazing at the final resting place of an ancestor whom you never knew: when I eventually identified my great-great-grandfather's grave, surrounded by those of his wife's family, in an overgrown country churchyard, for instance, I almost felt that I should introduce myself and helpfully explain my line of descent from him! Whether or not you have the sensation that someone is looking down on you with interest from another realm, you will probably feel a heightened sense of family connection and a renewed awareness of your ancestry, which will sharpen your powers of observation. The location and appearance of the grave will tell you something about your family's social and financial standing, as well as either their taste or the prevalent funerary style of the era in which their relations died. Although you should take photographs of the burial site as an *aide-memoire*, your photographic skills, camera, or film may prove unequal to cap-

turing the necessary detail, which is why it's far more important to make a written note of how the grave appeared and of the words that comprise any inscription. You could also make a rubbing of the gravestone, a method that can be particularly revealing if the inscription chiseled into a headstone has been eroded by time and the weather.

In summary, before venturing to a family graveyard, make sure that you are equipped with a camera, a pen and notebook, and perhaps also some large sheets of paper and a selection of soft-lead pencils, sticks of chalk, or pastels for rubbings. If you suspect that the burial site may have lain neglected for many years, it might be helpful to prepare a selection of cleaning materials, such as a soft-bristled scrubbing brush, a pail, and a bottle of water, with which to remove any moss or dirt that may be obscuring the inscription. A final item that you could add to your checklist may be a flowering plant or spray of fresh flowers to place on the grave in tribute to your enduring ancestral ties with the person or people who rest there.

You can learn a lot simply from the appearance of a family grave. Only an affluent family would have been able to afford to commission a marble angel like this to watch over a loved one.

RECORD OF FAMILY GRAVES

NAME	DATE OF DEATH	LOCATION	NOTES

PRESERVING AND CATALOGING YOUR FAMILY ARCHIVE

Having culled as much information as you can from family sources, before proceeding any further with your research you should assimilate what you have collected and learned and begin to catalog and collate your data. If organization is not your forte, this may not sound an appealing prospect, but it's nevertheless necessary, first to ensure that any original material that has come into your hands is safely preserved and, secondly, to clarify your findings, as well as redefine your objectives, through the recording and classification processes.

By sending out a call for information to your relations, you will have effectively appointed yourself custodian of your family archive, a position that brings its own responsibility to both past and future generations, namely the preservation of your shared heritage. If you now hold any original documentation, paperwork, or photographs, it's crucial that you protect them from potential destruction by the ravages of time, environmental damage, accidental mishaps, or careless handling. Perhaps the best way to do this is to photocopy or scan them carefully or else to make a written inventory of both the items themselves and the information that they contain before either returning them to their owners or filing them away in a cabinet where they will remain undisturbed. You should never write on any original documents, but if you feel that you must, use the least damaging option of lightly annotating them with a soft pencil on the back. Likewise, avoid defacing documents by subjecting them to, for example, a hole-puncher, stapler, or even paper clips (metal ones especially, which may rust). Instead, either place them loosely in a box file or wrap them in newspaper and then store your archive—ideally flat—in a safe place that is neither too warm nor too humid. Remember, too, that if you wish to display photographs, they should be placed out of direct sunlight in order to prevent them from becoming faded.

Having safeguarded the future of your family's original paperwork, label your working copies with any details of identification that you think necessary, such as who holds the original, the date on which the copy was made, or the subjects of any photographs—in short, with any information that will aid your ongoing research or that will help to track down the original should you, or anyone who inherits your work, need to consult it in the future. And if the worst-case scenario comes to pass and the original is destroyed, at least you will have a record of its existence, appearance, and of the information that it imparted. The same labeling advice applies to written inventories or photographs of artifacts and gravestones, along with data stored on computer, audio, or video storage systems. Because errors of transcription or omission are all too easy to make, you could also take the precaution of copying any completed questionnaires or family-related letters that you received from your relatives (if you consider this unnecessary, at least make sure that you preserve the original items so that you can refer to them later if the need arises). It would be a dispiriting waste of the time and effort that you invested in procuring the information that you now possess if it were to be lost, for whatever reason.

You can store your records and copy documents in the wallet provided in this volume. If your collection becomes very large, you can file the copies separately and retain in the wallet copies of the records you refer to most frequently during your research.

With the essential groundwork done, the next step is to collate and write up the data that you have collected into a chronological family record (or records, if you are working on the history of more than one of the families from which you are descended), with you appearing at either the starting or end point. How you record your family history is up to you—and some ideas include presenting it as a family tree (see Chapter 2 for further guidance); writing it up in narrative form as a story that spans the generations; simply noting down the relevant names, places, and dates, perhaps using a card-index system or computer database; or a combination of these methods.

However basic or elaborate your chosen method, because sources sometimes contradict each other, it is vital to include evidence in support of the facts that you're recording. When, for example, you're recording the date of your grandparents' marriage, note alongside it the source that provided the date, be it a marriage certificate, an inscription on a wedding ring, or a letter your aunt has written advising you of the date from memory. This may sound pedantic, but once such details have been written down, they often assume quasi-factual status, yet your aunt's memory may have been hazy and you may later find that the "fact" that she supplied is contradicted by another, more authoritative, source. Having a record of the provenance of the initial date will enable you to decide later whether the subsequent source is more reliable, and thus which of the two dates is probably the correct one. Keep the statements made by both sources on file, however, because a third source may later suggest that your aunt was right after all and that the second date was the result of a clerical error.

Although you could do it longhand, by far the most efficient way of transcribing and preserving your data is keying it into a computer. A multitude of PC- and Mac-based software programs dedicated to genealogy proliferate today, most of whose many time-saving functions include their ability automatically to draw up family trees, work out degrees of relationship, and present the same information in a variety of formats. Whether or not you use one of these or a conventional word-processing or database program, a computer's software will not only enable you to print out multiple copies of a file at the click of a mouse (a useful feature if you've promised to keep your relations abreast of your discoveries), but amend, or add to, your record without repeatedly having to undertake the tedious process of updating or rewriting your original version by hand as information comes to light. Computers have further advantages, too: they enable you to access the growing number of websites devoted to family history, while computer scanners offer a convenient method of reproducing and storing photographs and documents. Of course, a computer is simply a tool and not a necessity, but you will find it an extremely efficient and convenient one if you find that you've been bitten by the family-history bug. If you do use a computer, remember that both hard- and software are notoriously prone to glitches and crashes, so always back up your data regularly and keep hard copies of your computer files. The hard copies will also be accessible for your descendents to read long after your software has become outdated!

However you decide to collate your data, organization is vital if you are to avoid becoming thoroughly confused when trying to work out which pieces of your family-history puzzle fit into the correct slots, as well as ensuring that you do not mislay snippets of information, particularly if you are working on more than one family. Even if you are concentrating on your father's paternal line of descent, you'll probably still have amassed some information on his mother's family—and your own mother's—which you're unlikely to want to consign to the trash, whether or not you intend to investigate them further at a later stage. The most important basic organizational strategy is therefore to dedicate a file to each family segment (and perhaps even two, one containing your source material and detailed biographies of your forebears, along with any other more peripheral, but still pertinent, information, and the other the record of your line of descent, be it in the form of a narrative chronicle or a graphic family tree, or both). Segregating your families in such a way will make the information specific to one far easier to locate than if their records were stored in a single, jumbled file, as well as enabling you to keep track of your progress through history at a glance.

SUMMARY OF RECORDS COLLATED

FAMILY QUESTIONNAIRES

NAME	DATE RECORDED	COMMENTS/NOTES

NOTES

INDIVIDUALS, EVENTS, OR RECORDS TO FOLLOW UP FROM FAMILY QUESTIONNAIRE RESPONSES

DOCUMENTS LOCATED

	NAME	LOCATION OF ORIGINAL	COPIES MADE
BIRTH CERTIFICATES:			
MARRIAGE CERTIFICATES:			
DEATH CERTIFICATES:			
EMPLOYMENT RECORDS:			
RELIGIOUS RECORDS:			
MILITARY RECORDS:			
IMMIGRATION RECORDS:			
PASSPORTS/TRAVEL DOCS:			

PHOTOGRAPHS AND FAMILY HEIRLOOMS

DESCRIPTION	LOCATION OF ORIGINAL	COMMENTS/NOTES

From Acorn to Oak Tree

Some Ways of Displaying Your Family Tree

The term "family tree" is an apt one, for just as an acorn germinates into a seedling, sending out roots deep into the earth before producing the branches and twigs that proclaim its status as a fully fledged oak tree—in turn a producer of acorns—so each of us is both the progeny and potential progenitor of an extensive family network.

The tree is exalted as a powerful symbol of cosmic regeneration in the myths and religions of many cultures. The world tree of Norse mythology, for example, was an ash named Yggdrasil, whose roots encompassed the underworld realms, whose trunk was home to the mortals, and whose lofty branches supported the divine domain of the gods. And although the nine teeming worlds housed by Yggdrasil were doomed to be destroyed at the apocalyptic battle of Ragnarok, from its trunk, it is told, would spring two seeds that would germinate into a man and woman, who would together repopulate the world's human family.

Among the oldest representations of a family tree is the Jesse Tree that is depicted in the windows of many Christian churches, which traces Christ's descent from Jesse through Jesse's son, King David, to Christ's mother, the Virgin Mary, as foretold in the Old Testament Book of Isaiah (11:1–2): "There shall come forth a rod out of the stem of Jesse, and a branch shall grow out of his roots and the Spirit of the Lord shall rest upon him." Jesse is typically depicted lying at the bottom of this messianic pedigree, with the resurrected Christ appearing at its apex, thereby emulating how a living tree's roots (and it's no accident that we refer to our family lineage as our "roots") support its vigorous crown. The pattern set by the Jesse Tree is just one of the many ways in which a family's line of descent can be portrayed in graphic form.

Perhaps the best-recognized type of family tree is the drop-line tree (effectively an inverted Jesse Tree) or descendant chart, with the ancestral father and mother of the family appearing at the top of the tree and each successive generation then dropping a line in turn, so that the most recent family members are ranged across the bottom. An example is shown overleaf. Although it is easy to trace your line of descent using this format, a practical problem is that if each of the generations descended from the original ancestral pairing comprises many members, like a pyramid, the base will be far wider than the apex—so wide, in fact, that it may not fit onto a single page. In addition, because a comprehensive family tree consisting of the descendants of all of your forebears would soon become crowded out with individuals, when working with this format, it's best to create a separate drop-line tree for each of your core families, that is, your father's, mother's, paternal grandmother's, maternal grandmother's, and so on.

If the top-to-bottom drop-line family tree doesn't suit the ancestral information that you want to record, an alternative is the left-to-right tree known as an ancestors' birth brief (also called a multigeneration or pedigree chart), in which your family history is read from left to right, much as a book is read, with you on the left (numbered 1) as the starting point; your father (numbered 2) slightly to your right and above you and your mother (numbered 3) slightly to your right and below you; the same layout being applied to their parents, who should therefore appear slightly to the right, respectively above and below, their children, as well as to their parents, parents' parents, and so on. Your father's father

 Trees feature in many of the world's creation stories. In the Judeo-Christian Old Testament Book of Genesis, for example, it is told that the untroubled existence of Adam and Eve, the ancestors of humankind, in the Garden of Eden came to a bitter end when Eve succumbed to the temptation to taste the forbidden fruit of the tree of knowledge of good and evil.

DROP-LINE TREE

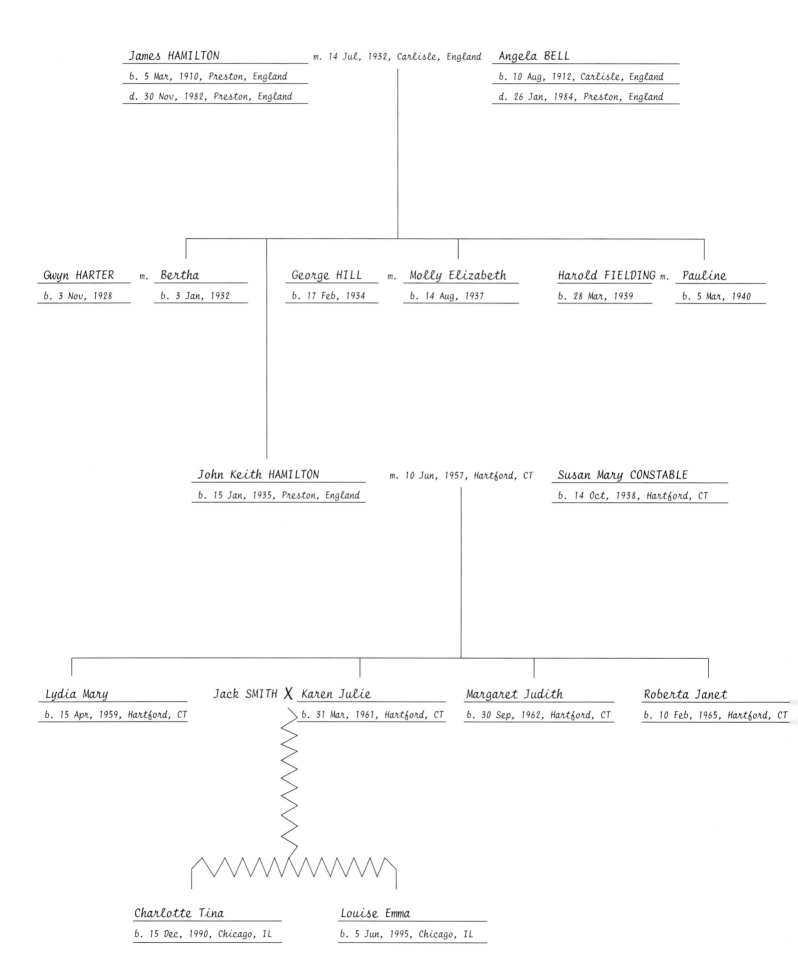

James HAMILTON   m. 14 Jul, 1932, Carlisle, England   Angela BELL

b. 5 Mar, 1910, Preston, England   b. 10 Aug, 1912, Carlisle, England

d. 30 Nov, 1982, Preston, England   d. 26 Jan, 1984, Preston, England

Gwyn HARTER   m.   Bertha   George HILL   m.   Molly Elizabeth   Harold FIELDING m.   Pauline

b. 3 Nov, 1928   b. 3 Jan, 1932   b. 17 Feb, 1934   b. 14 Aug, 1937   b. 28 Mar, 1939   b. 5 Mar, 1940

John Keith HAMILTON   m. 10 Jun, 1957, Hartford, CT   Susan Mary CONSTABLE

b. 15 Jan, 1935, Preston, England   b. 14 Oct, 1938, Hartford, CT

Lydia Mary   Jack SMITH X Karen Julie   Margaret Judith   Roberta Janet

b. 15 Apr, 1959, Hartford, CT   b. 31 Mar, 1961, Hartford, CT   b. 30 Sep, 1962, Hartford, CT   b. 10 Feb, 1965, Hartford, CT

Charlotte Tina   Louise Emma

b. 15 Dec, 1990, Chicago, IL   b. 5 Jun, 1995, Chicago, IL

ABOUT MY FAMILY

My full name is ....

I was born on .... in ....

My occupation is ....

My interests are ....

My father's full name is ....

He was born on .... in ....

My mother's full name is ....

She was born on .... in ....

They were married on .... at ....

My siblings are ....

....

....

My spouse's name is ....

He/she was born on .... in ....

We were married on .... at ....

His/her occupaiton is ....

His/her interest are ....

Our children are ....

....

....

Our pets are ....

We live in ....

Our grandchildren are ....

....

....

My best friends are ....

My ambition or dream is ....

My motto or philosophy of life is ....

I would like to be remembered as ....

....

....

My Family Portrait

Names: ....

....

....

....

Place/event: ....

Date: ....

MY FAMILY TREE

❧

⌐⌐ ⌐⌐ *The cut-out-and-keep family tree. Use the space opposite for a group family photograph, recording underneath the names of those pictured, the place or event, and the date of the photograph.*

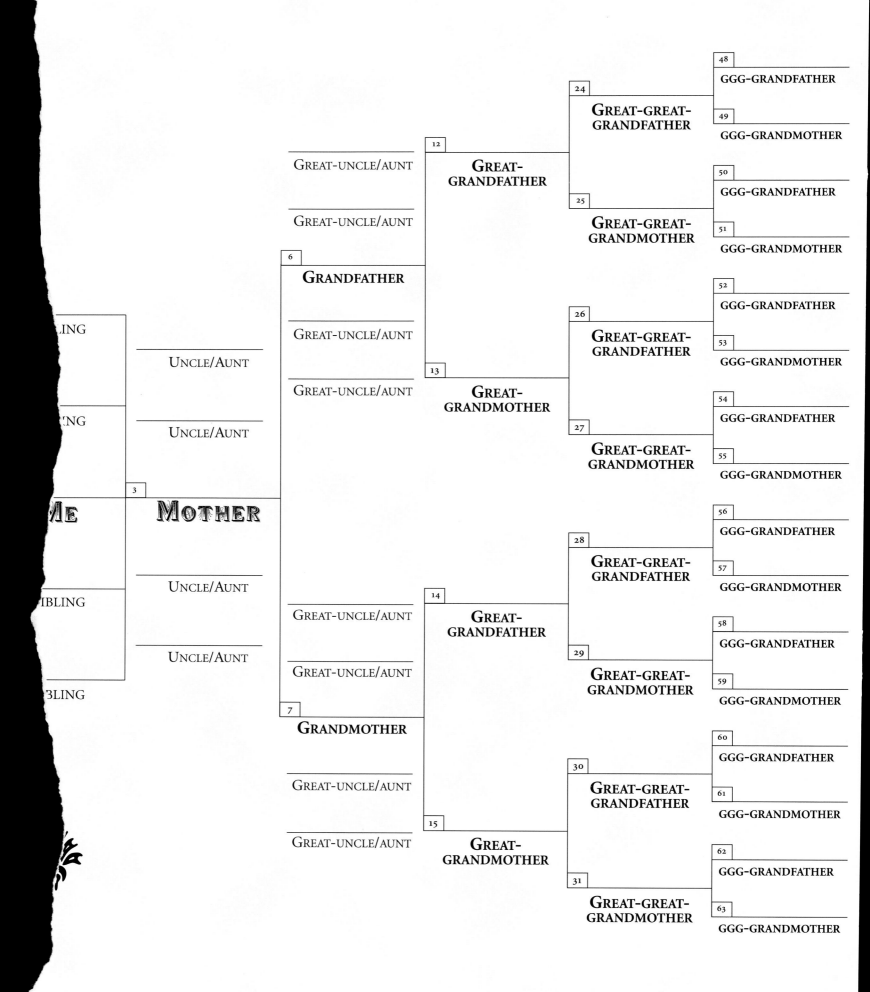

MILY TREE

48 GGG-GRANDFATHER

24 GREAT-GREAT-GRANDFATHER

49 GGG-GRANDMOTHER

12 GREAT-GRANDFATHER

50 GGG-GRANDFATHER

25 GREAT-GREAT-GRANDMOTHER

51 GGG-GRANDMOTHER

GREAT-UNCLE/AUNT

GREAT-UNCLE/AUNT

6 GRANDFATHER

52 GGG-GRANDFATHER

26 GREAT-GREAT-GRANDFATHER

53 GGG-GRANDMOTHER

GREAT-UNCLE/AUNT

13 GREAT-GRANDMOTHER

54 GGG-GRANDFATHER

GREAT-UNCLE/AUNT

27 GREAT-GREAT-GRANDMOTHER

55 GGG-GRANDMOTHER

LING

ING

UNCLE/AUNT

UNCLE/AUNT

3 MOTHER

ME

56 GGG-GRANDFATHER

28 GREAT-GREAT-GRANDFATHER

57 GGG-GRANDMOTHER

14 GREAT-GRANDFATHER

58 GGG-GRANDFATHER

29 GREAT-GREAT-GRANDMOTHER

59 GGG-GRANDMOTHER

UNCLE/AUNT

IBLING

UNCLE/AUNT

GREAT-UNCLE/AUNT

GREAT-UNCLE/AUNT

BLING

7 GRANDMOTHER

60 GGG-GRANDFATHER

30 GREAT-GREAT-GRANDFATHER

61 GGG-GRANDMOTHER

GREAT-UNCLE/AUNT

15 GREAT-GRANDMOTHER

62 GGG-GRANDFATHER

GREAT-UNCLE/AUNT

31 GREAT-GREAT-GRANDMOTHER

63 GGG-GRANDMOTHER

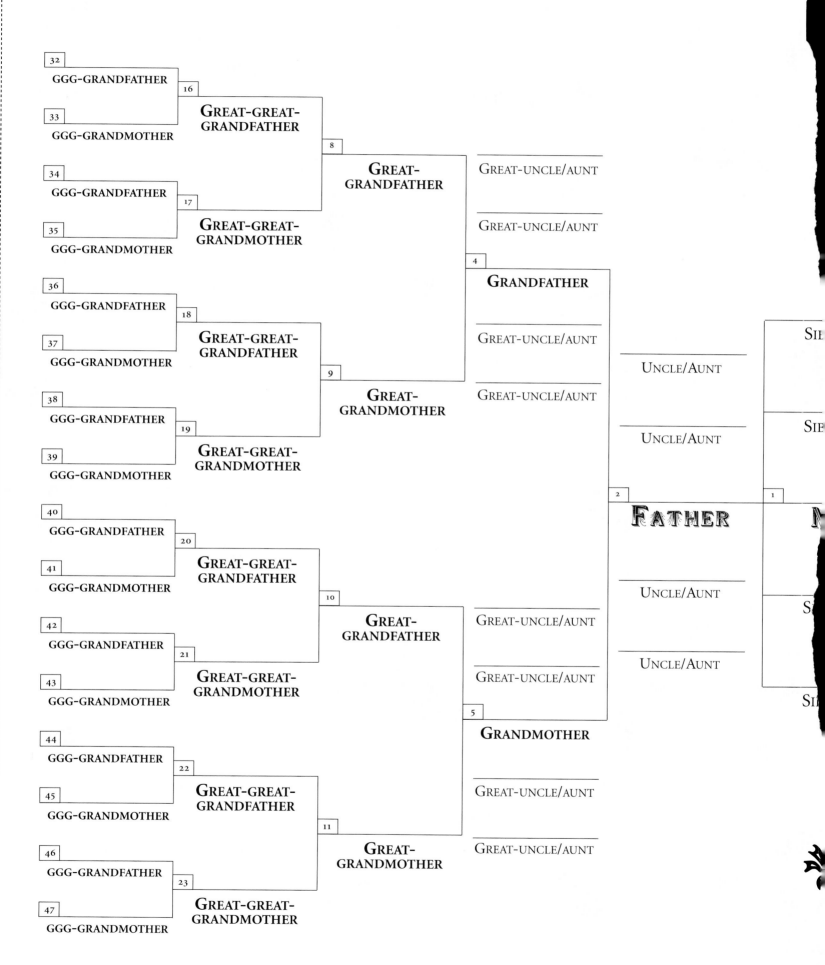

32
GGG-GRANDFATHER

16
GREAT-GREAT-GRANDFATHER

33
GGG-GRANDMOTHER

8
GREAT-GRANDFATHER

34
GGG-GRANDFATHER

17
GREAT-GREAT-GRANDMOTHER

35
GGG-GRANDMOTHER

GREAT-UNCLE/AUNT

GREAT-UNCLE/AUNT

4
GRANDFATHER

36
GGG-GRANDFATHER

18
GREAT-GREAT-GRANDFATHER

37
GGG-GRANDMOTHER

GREAT-UNCLE/AUNT

9
GREAT-GRANDMOTHER

GREAT-UNCLE/AUNT

38
GGG-GRANDFATHER

19
GREAT-GREAT-GRANDMOTHER

39
GGG-GRANDMOTHER

UNCLE/AUNT

UNCLE/AUNT

SIB

SIB

2
FATHER

1
M

40
GGG-GRANDFATHER

20
GREAT-GREAT-GRANDFATHER

41
GGG-GRANDMOTHER

10
GREAT-GRANDFATHER

GREAT-UNCLE/AUNT

42
GGG-GRANDFATHER

21
GREAT-GREAT-GRANDMOTHER

43
GGG-GRANDMOTHER

GREAT-UNCLE/AUNT

UNCLE/AUNT

UNCLE/AUNT

5
GRANDMOTHER

44
GGG-GRANDFATHER

22
GREAT-GREAT-GRANDFATHER

45
GGG-GRANDMOTHER

GREAT-UNCLE/AUNT

SIB

11
GREAT-GRANDMOTHER

GREAT-UNCLE/AUNT

46
GGG-GRANDFATHER

23
GREAT-GREAT-GRANDMOTHER

47
GGG-GRANDMOTHER

ANCESTORS' BIRTH BRIEF

8	Jeremiah HAMILTON
	b. 1883, Preston, England
	m. ?
	k.i.a. 1916, Somme, France

4	James HAMILTON
	b. 5 Mar, 1910, Preston, England
	m. 14 Jul, 1932, Carlisle, England
	d. 30 Nov, 1982, Preston, England

9	Daisy May CARTER
	b. ?
	d. 1941, Preston, England

2	John Keith HAMILTON
	b. 15 Jan, 1935, Preston, England
	m. 10 Jun, 1957, Hartford, CT

10	John BELL
	b. 1891, Carlisle, England
	m. 12 Apr, 1910, Carlisle, England
	d. ?

5	Angela BELL
	b. 10 Aug, 1912, Carlisle, England
	d. 26 Jan, 1984, Preston, England

11	Marion FOX
	b. ?
	d. 1952, Carlisle, England

1	Margaret Judith HAMILTON
	b. 30 Sep, 1962, Hartford, CT

12	Edward CONSTABLE
	b. 1881
	m. ?
	d. 1939, Burnley, England

6	Alfred CONSTABLE
	b. 20 Feb, 1905, Burnley, England
	m. 5 Aug, 1933, Burnley, England
	d. 11 Sep, 1965, Burnley, England

13	?
	b. ?
	d. ?

3	Susan Mary
	b. 14 Oct, 1938, Hartford, CT

14	George LANCASTER
	b. 1881
	m. ?
	d. ?

7	Emily LANCASTER
	b. 25 Jul, 1908, Burnley, England
	d. 2 Dec, 1974, Lancaster, England

15	Lucy HARTLEY
	b. 1887, Burnley, England
	d. ?

should be numbered 4 and your father's mother 5, while your mother's father should be numbered 6 and your mother's mother 7, the numbers increasing in the same way with the generations, from which pattern you can discern that fathers are given even numbers and mothers odd ones. An example of this kind of tree is shown on the previous page.

One of the advantages of this *Ahnentafel* (a German word meaning "table of ancestors") numbering system is that if you have additional biographical information relating to the individuals who appear on your family tree, assigning each a number that is unique to him or her and labeling the file in which their biographies are stored with the same number makes cross-referencing less confusing, particularly if two or more people share the same first and family names. Another is that you can quickly identify the father of an individual by doubling the individual's number (so that the father of person number 2 will be person number 4) and the mother by doubling the individual's number and adding one (so that the mother of person number 2 will be person number 5).

As its name indicates, an ancestors' birth brief comprises your direct ancestors only, not their siblings, as do two further ways of displaying a family tree, the semicircular and circular formats (with you in the center and your direct ancestors radiating outward in successive waves). Although you may not wish to restrict yourself to recording your direct ancestry alone, it's nevertheless advisable to draw up your pedigree in this way to give you an instant point of reference and to supple-

ment it with a drop-line chart (or charts) that includes all of your known relations.

If you want to include as much information as possible within multiple records of your descent, other ways of charting your ancestry, albeit in nongraphic form, include person or individual sheets, which include all of the information that is known about one individual; family group sheets, which summarize the vital details of a father, mother, and their children; *Ahnentafel* reports, which present pedigrees in written form; and chronological profiles, which list family events in the order in which they occurred. An additional option is a descent-format tree, a purely textual listing in which the ultimate male ancestor appears at top left and each successive generation is assigned a number, the names of its members being indented farther and farther to the right as the generational numbers increase. This often proves an initially confusing format for the uninitiated to make sense of, however.

None of these formats is more correct than another, and your choice should therefore be dictated either by your personal preference or by which best suits the number of names, or amount of information relating to them, that you want to accommodate. Unless you've invested in a genealogical software package, however, most of which give you the option of experimenting with a number of automatically generated styles of display after you've entered your family details into its database, you'll probably find a drop-line tree or ancestors' birth brief the easiest format to create and work with when you're starting out.

The numbering system for your line of descent explained in detail. You can record your numbered ancestors in the chart on page 61.

WHO'S WHO IN THE NUMBERED TREE

1 Myself	7 My mother's mother	13 My mother's father's mother
2 My father	8 My father's father's father	14 My mother's mother's father
3 My mother	9 My father's father's mother	15 My mother's mother's mother
4 My father's father	10 My father's mother's father	16 My father's father's father's father
5 My father's mother	11 My father's mother's mother	17 My father's father's father's mother
6 My mother's father	12 My mother's father's father	18 My father's father's mother's father

DRAWING UP YOUR FAMILY TREE

Whichever your preferred family-tree format, there are a few rules that will help anyone who sees it instantly to make sense of your family tree, as well as enable you to keep track of who's who, what happened to them, and when and how they're related to you.

Under each person's full name (write the family name in capital letters), record the vital dates that chart the course of his or her life in chronological order—birth, baptism or christening (both optional), marriage, divorce (if applicable), death, and burial (optional)—as well as the place at which each event occurred. You could also include additional biographical information, such as religion, educational achievements, and profession, but this will make your family tree look overly cluttered. It is simpler and clearer to preserve such information elsewhere and to use the numerical cross-referencing system outlined above to link an individual with the relevant data.

If you are unsure whether a date is correct, indicate your uncertainty by inserting an appropriate qualifier, such as an abbreviation (see the list of abbreviations below) denoting "*circa*," "before," "after," or "probably." An alternative is to insert a question mark (particularly if you have no information at all) or, if more than one claimant presents itself for a name, date, or place, all of the competing candidates.

Decide which format you prefer for recording dates and stick to it. Most family historians agree that the least ambiguous method is not the numerical month/day/year style (3/1/2001), but the day/month/year alternative, for example, either 1 March, 2001, or 1/III/2001 (spelling out the month or using Roman numerals limits the potential for confusion). In addition, don't abbreviate the year, but always write it in full (for instance, 2001, not '01). Similarly, be consistent when using abbreviations to avoid confusion.

Always give a married woman's maiden name as her family name, not her husband's.

Draw a line from the marriage abbreviation or symbol to link married parents with their children (or a wavy or zigzag line to link unmarried parents with their children). If a child was adopted, it is generally not linked to its adoptive parents by a line, a tree's primary purpose being usually to chart a family's bloodline (see pages 91–92).

If parents have more than one child, record them in order of birth, that is, the eldest child first and the youngest last.

Although the family name should always be included after each male child's given name, many genealogists advocate that only the given names of female children should be entered (this convention may seem sexist, but it delineates a line of descent more clearly).

Display the members of the same generation on the same line or level and link groups of siblings with a straight line, unless they are illegitimate, in which case use a wavy line.

Overleaf ☞☞ *A sample person sheet and family group sheet. Use copies of these to record more information about people in your family. The notes section on the person sheet can be used to record details of military service, addresses, sources of information, documents that you have located, godparents, or any other useful notes.*

BASIC GENEALOGICAL ABBREVIATIONS AND SYMBOLS

BORN: **b.** or **bn.** or **brn.**

BAPTIZED: **bap.** or **bapt.**

CHRISTENED: **c.** or **chr.** (but note that **c.** could be confused with *circa*)

MARRIED: **m.** or **mar.** or **marr.** or **=** (between the couple's names)

DIED: **d.** or **dd.** or **ob.** or **obit.**

KILLED IN ACTION: **k.i.a.**

BURIED: **bd.** or **bu.** or **bur.**

FEMALE: **F.**

MALE: **M.**

ILLEGITIMATE: **illeg.**

ADOPTED: **adop.**

UNMARRIED PARENTS: **x** (inserted between the couple's names)

DIVORCED: **div.**

FIRST WIFE OR HUSBAND: **(1)** (inserted before the relevant name, which should be placed

to the left of that of the husband or wife) or **m.1.** (placed before the name).

SECOND WIFE OR HUSBAND: **(2)** (inserted before the relevant name, to the right of the husband or wife) or **m.2.**

DATE UNCERTAIN: **c.** or **ca.** (both abbreviations of *circa*)

PROBABLY: **prob.**

PERSON SHEET   NAME: NUMBER:

Name: ☐ ....

Date and place of birth: ....

Baptism/christening: ....

Religion: ....

Occupation: ....

Father's name: ....

Mother's name: ....

Date and place of death: ....

Burial place: ....

Spouse(s) Name: ☐ ....

Date and place of birth: ....

Baptism/christening: ....

Religion: ....

Occupation: ....

Father's name: ....

Mother's name: ....

Date and place of marriage: ....

Children's names: ☐ ....

☐ ....

☐ ....

Date and place of death: ....

Burial place: ....

Notes: ....

....

....

....

....

....

FAMILY GROUP SHEET

NAME: **NUMBER:**

.... ☐

Husband's name

....

His father's name

....

His mother's name

.... ☐

Wife's name

....

Her father's name

....

Her mother's name

Date of birth:	....
Place of birth:	....
Date of death:	....
Cause of death:	....
Place of death:	....
Where buried:	....
Marriage date:	....
Marriage place:	....
Date of birth:	....
Place of birth:	....
Date of death:	....
Cause of death:	....
Place of death:	....
Where buried:	....

Children	Date and place of birth	Date and place of marriage	Spouse's name	Date and place of death
☐ Name				
☐ Name				
☐ Name				
☐ Name				
☐ Name				

Notes: ....

....

....

EMBELLISHING YOUR FAMILY TREE

Once you've drafted and then drawn up your family tree, you could bring it to life by accompanying each name (or as many as you are able) with a photograph of the individual. If photographs of your ancestors are lacking, however, an alternative is to use a graphic symbol with which to denote a person's profession or consuming interest: a sailboat or anchor for a sailor, for example; a needle and thread for an accomplished seamstress; or a teddy bear for someone whose life was cut short in childhood. Should your family have been granted a coat of arms and motto, you could display it above your line of descent, as you could the badge of the clan to which your family belongs if your ancestry is rooted in Scotland or, indeed, any other symbol associated with your family. And if you prefer not to include pictorial or graphic illustrations within your family tree, you could still enhance its clarity and interest by the use of color: for instance, by assigning black to names and connecting lines and red to dates and place names; you could in addition unite members of each generation by enclosing their names within color-coded boxes, perhaps using blue for the first generation, yellow for the second, green for the third, and so on. Several genealogical software programs offer color-coding functions, as well as the ability to insert scanned images at the appropriate points in family trees; some even offer a timeline with which to set your forebears' lives in historical context by displaying them alongside events of national and international sig-

nificance. If you do not have access to such automated software facilities, or would derive greater satisfaction from immersing yourself in the old-fashioned process of designing and making an illustrated family tree yourself, however, arm yourself with some scissors, glue, a pencil and eraser, and a selection of colored pens. Remember that because creating a family tree by hand will involve many trial-and-error attempts, you'll probably also need lots of sheets of paper to experiment on before you arrive at your final version, and for the same reason it would be a wise precaution to make a number of photocopies of the images that you intend to include to lessen the chances of inadvertently spoiling your original documents and illustrations.

Finally, when you're satisfied that you can improve your design no further, a color photocopier can provide near-perfect duplicates of your family tree to present to other family members, perhaps as a token of your gratitude for any information that they gave you that helped you to compile it. Be warned, however, that reviewing the results of your painstaking work may cause the recipients suddenly to recall a few more names that should have been included in your family tree, in which case you'll have to go back to the drawing board or computer keyboard. Indeed, it's very unlikely that you'll be able to produce a definitive family tree first time round, and it will probably always have work-in-progress status. As you discover new sources, you may continue to add more details through your own research, but then the knowledge that there is always unfinished family business to be worked on is one of the many joys of pursuing genealogy.

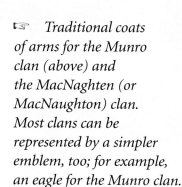

☞ *Traditional coats of arms for the Munro clan (above) and the MacNaghten (or MacNaughton) clan. Most clans can be represented by a simpler emblem, too; for example, an eagle for the Munro clan.*

MY LINE OF DESCENT
FOR FIVE GENERATIONS

Name	Group Sheet Names & Numbers
1 Myself	
2 My father	
3 My mother	
4 My father's father	
5	
6	
7	
8	
9	
10	
11	
12	
13	
14	
15	
16	
17	
18	
19	
20	
21	
22	
23	
24	
25	
26	
27	
28	
29	
30	
31	

Tracking Down Your Ancestors

Once you have gathered as much information about your shared family history as your relations can provide, drawing up a family tree based on the results of your initial trawl for information will, no doubt, have revealed some missing links in your ancestral chain, as well as an absence of vital data for certain individuals. Your next port of call should now be the institutions that hold the records that may help you to fill in the gaps, that is, those whose archives contain birth, marriage, and death records, details of baptisms and burials, and census returns. For, in the words of the French writer Jean Giraudoux, "Government defines the physical aspects of man by means of The Printed Form, so that for every man in the flesh [and, one could add, the men, women, and children whose flesh has since become dust] there is an exactly corresponding man on paper." (*The Enchanted*, 1933).

When you start to pursue the paper trail, most family historians advocate targeting the recorded events that mark the rites of passage of your forebears' lives in reverse order, that is, locating death or burial details first, followed by marriage records, and, finally, birth certificates or baptismal records. This advice is partly based on the need to verify the identity of an individual named in the records. For example, if you know that a person named in a death certificate was definitely your grandmother, the date of her death in combination with her age at death will help you to estimate her likely birth date if this is not given or is otherwise unknown to you. It may confirm such details as her full name and birth place, and perhaps even parentage—all invaluable aids when both searching for a birth certificate and/or confirming identity. In addition, there is the practical consideration of whether some vital records even exist: unlike in England and Wales, whose civil records of births, marriages, and deaths began on July 1, 1837, in the United States civil registration was typically only officially instituted at state level at around the end of the nineteenth century and the start of the twentieth (although New England is an exception). The dates when the civil registration of vital events became compulsory vary widely around the world, and, as a general rule, the later the likely date of the documentation for which you are searching, the easier it will be to locate, so that a death certificate will usually be less difficult to track down than a birth certificate. However, if you intend to consult a particular archive, engaging in a blanket search—that is, identifying all of the vital events connected with a certain family name—often proves as fruitful as selective targeting. This approach may result in your puzzling over some misfits, but keep their details on file, because further research may reveal them to be ancestral fits.

In recent decades, searching for the records of baptisms (which, in the case of babies, indicate the year of birth) and marriages has been greatly facilitated by the public release of the records gathered by the Church of Jesus Christ of Latter-day Saints (L.D.S.) since 1894. Originally begun to assist its members to identify their ancestors so that they could be posthumously received into the church, the benefit to genealogists of the L.D.S.'s ongoing program has been the centralization of the records of scores of religious denominations from all over the world within the International Genealogical Index (I.G.I.). Although the I.G.I. currently contains around 600 million names, the recording process remains not only incomplete, but occasionally inaccurate, yet it is still an extremely useful tool. This source may at

 Harold Gibson and Rose Patterson pictured on September 3, 1923, after their marriage at Saint Thomas's Roman Catholic Church, in the bride's home town of Canterbury, in the English county of Kent. Rose's parents' marriage certificate appears on page 69, below that of Harold's grandparents.

least give you initial information that you can later verify or amend through consulting alternative sources, some of which the I.G.I. will direct you to.

Brigham Young's Cabinet

Supplementing vital records, census returns usually contain a mine of circumstantial evidence, as well as giving you a set of intriguing snapshots of your family's changing group dynamics and fortunes over the years. Gaining access to these will provide you with all sorts of information that you may not be able to uncover if you restrict yourself to vital records. This can include the existence of children that were hitherto unknown to you; the size of forebears' households; and their occupations. And if you have no success in tracking down documentary proof of a forebear's birth, marriage, or death, examining both religious and census records may help you to fill in some missing pieces of your family-history puzzle.

This chapter gives an overview of how such family records can further your research, but because listing all of the county, state, national, and international sources for such information would require a book in itself, it can only point you in the likely general direction of those that may hold vital data pertaining to your family. This is the point at which you'll have to launch yourself into family detection, so put on your deerstalker, pick up your magnifying glass, and prepare to start sleuthing.

BIRTH CERTIFICATES

"In the early days of the Indian Territory, there were no such things as birth certificates. You being there was certificate enough," as Will Rogers, the U.S. actor, humorist, and newspaper columnist, wryly, but accurately, observed in 1962. Indeed, it was not until the late nineteenth and early twentieth centuries that the bureaucracies of many U.S. states began to require the arrival of newborns to be registered officially, making tracking down the birth records of U.S. citizens a less straightforward process than those born in England and Wales, Scotland (whose program of civil registration began in 1858), and Ireland (from 1864), for example. For information on American births, the first step is therefore to note down the state,

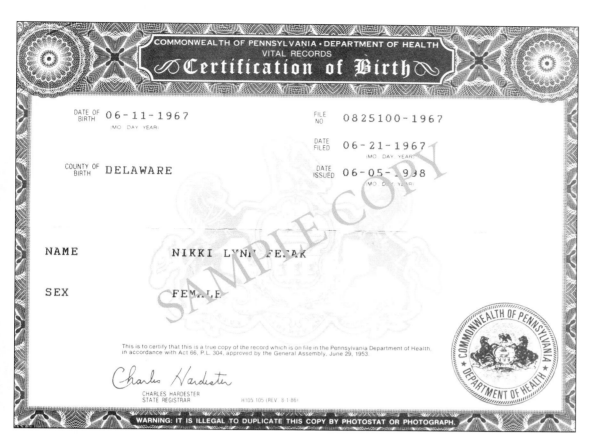

COMMONWEALTH OF PENNSYLVANIA · DEPARTMENT OF HEALTH
VITAL RECORDS
Certification of Birth

DATE OF BIRTH 06-11-1967
(MO DAY YEAR)

FILE NO 0825100-1967

DATE FILED 06-21-1967
(MO DAY YEAR)

COUNTY OF BIRTH DELAWARE

DATE ISSUED 06-05-1938
(MO DAY YEAR)

NAME NIKKI LYNN FETAK

SEX FEMALE

This is to certify that this is a true copy of the record which is on file in the Pennsylvania Department of Health, in accordance with Act 66, P.L. 304, approved by the General Assembly, June 29, 1953.

Charles Hardester
CHARLES HARDESTER
STATE REGISTRAR

H105 105 (REV 8·1·86)

WARNING: IT IS ILLEGAL TO DUPLICATE THIS COPY BY PHOTOSTAT OR PHOTOGRAPH.

▨ *Relatively recent certifications of birth in the United States provide the subject's full name, sex, date of birth, county and state of birth, and the date on which the birth details were filed, along with the file reference number. Many states prohibit the release of such certificates if it is likely that the person in question is still alive, that is, unless you are applying for a copy of your own birth certificate.*

states, or country in which you believe each of your ancestors was born, along with their dates of birth (or estimated birth dates), and then to find out when those states or nations began to record vital information. (If you have Internet access, www.vitalrec.com gives state-by-state details; alternatively, refer to the list of useful publications on page 97.) If any entries on your list of ancestral births took place thereafter, there's a good chance that you will be able to obtain their birth certificates. An important point to note, however, is that some states adhere to a strict privacy policy restricting the release of vital records, particularly those that may relate to people who are still alive. For English and Welsh births, the Family Records Centre in London holds an index of births from 1837 (see pages 100–01 for further details, and for starting points in other countries).

Birth certificates are useful for the family-history researcher not only because they provide a full name and birth date for the child, but they also usually state the name of his or her father, thereby taking you back a generation. The later the date of the birth certificate, the more details relating to the

child's parents will be included, so that you may receive a document giving the child's full name, gender, ethnic group, and date and place of birth, along with the names and birthplaces of both parents, their ages when the child was born, the number of children to whom the mother had already given birth, and how many of those children were alive when their latest sibling was born. Records more than one hundred years old usually contain far less information, however: perhaps only the child's name, date of birth, and father's name (although that of the mother is sometimes also specified). Reflecting those more parochial times, note, too, that the place of birth may not be specified when it was registered at the courthouse of the town in which the child was born, but may appear in county records.

When researching a twentieth-century birth in the United States, if you know the exact name, date, and place of birth of the person whose certificate you require, the fastest way of obtaining it is usually to contact the courthouse of the town, or clerk's office of the county, in which the birth took place to request verification of the event, as

▨▨ *Laying out your family tree would pose a real challenge if you were a descendant of Brigham Young, the polygamous nineteenth-century Mormon leader depicted here with a "cabinet" of thirty-six wives (the actual figure was twenty-seven). Young fathered fifty-seven children. He founded Salt Lake City, where the L.D.S.'s Family History Library Building is today located.*

According to his birth certificate, John Townend Gibson (the father of the bridegroom portrayed on page 62) was born on April 9, 1861, in Grainthorpe, in the registration district of Louth, in the subdistrict of Tetney, in the English county of Lincoln. His parents are named as John Westmorland Gibson, a farmer, and Charlotte Gibson, formerly Mamwell, who registered the birth on April 26, 1861. Copies of English birth certificates are always printed on red paper.

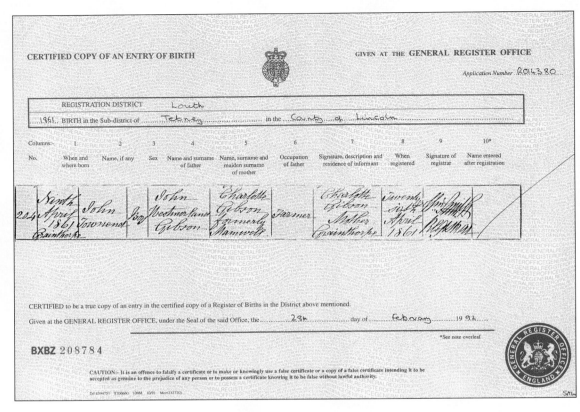

well as information on how to obtain further details. Alternatively, if your ancestor's birth details are less clear-cut, indexes listing the births registered within each state are usually held within the archives of the relevant state's vital-statistics office (typically located in the state capital), so once you have pinpointed the person's likely birth state, write to the archive of the state in question, enclosing as much information as you know about your forebear, such as his or her name, parentage, and probable date and place of birth, and inquiring whether a search could be undertaken. Your best chance of success when searching for birth details pertaining to the nineteenth century and earlier is to contact either the town (especially in New England) or county courthouse, but because some county records may have been lodged with the state archives, contacting the relevant state archive to ascertain their location is often a sensible place to begin.

Note that you will probably have to pay a fee for the archives to be searched, and, if the search is successful, for a copy of the birth certificate, which must sometimes be paid in advance. The policy of some state and courthouse archives prohibits their staff from undertaking searches on your behalf, however, in which case you'll have to conduct the search yourself, either by visiting the courthouse where the records are held or, if the records (or indexes to the records) have been transferred to microfilm or microfiche for distribution to those genealogical societies that have an interest in them, visiting one of those, either in person or over the Internet. Contact the relevant archive for further details. For English and Welsh births from 1837, you can visit the Family Records Centre in London to order birth-certificate copies after obtaining the relevant index reference, or, for a higher fee, apply for copies by mail from the Office for National Statistics (see page 100 for further details).

MARITAL RECORDS

As well as verifying that your great-grandparents, for instance, were indeed married, obtaining their marriage certificate may enable you to discover some important details that had previously eluded you, such as where and when the marriage ceremony took place or, perhaps more excitingly in terms of your research, your great-grandmother's maiden name, the magic key that may reveal an entirely new family to add to your ancestral tree.

For marriages in England and Wales, information, indexes, and certificate copies are available from the sources outlined above for births. In the United States, there are two types of official marital document that may shed further light on your family history: bonds and licenses. Prior to the twentieth century, a prospective bridegroom was often required to post a bond guaranteeing that if the marriage subsequently proved to be illegal for any reason, a fine would be paid to the colonial or state government to cover the cost of nullification and any resulting litigation, someone else (usually a friend or relation of the bride) in addition being required to stand surety for the sum. Depending on the state in which the wedding took place, the marriage license that eventually superseded the bond should at least provide the couple's full names and the dates on which the license was issued and returned to the courthouse to be filed, while many archived marriage records also include the date on which the marriage took place, along with the couple's ages, occupations, and the names of their parents, as well as occasionally detailing any witnesses (again typically kith and kin) to the event and the name of the presiding clergyman or judicial officer.

Because marriage certificates were usually given to couples as soon as they'd been pronounced man and wife, their descendants may have preserved them, but if they are no longer in your family's possession, it may be possible to discover documentary evidence of the marriage, that is, a bond or license, by contacting either the town or county courthouse or clerk's office in the locality where you believe the ceremony to have taken place or the relevant state's vital-statistics office for assistance (see the section on birth certificates for advice on how to do this).

You have two primary options when deciding which courthouse to approach:

firstly, if the bride and groom were living in the same neighborhood before their marriage, the courthouse whose area of jurisdiction covered the locality; or, secondly, if the couple lived in different places before their marriage, the courthouse local to the bride's place of residence before marriage. These strategies are generally successful if both parties were of the minimum age specified by the state (but note that the age varies from state to state) to render the marriage legal, or, in the case of an underage bride or groom (or both), if a parent or guardian had consented to the marriage and had given a sworn affidavit to that effect. The marriage trail may, however, be obscured if consent was refused, in which case the

🖼 *This charming photograph conveys the pride and happiness of a young couple on their wedding day. Obtaining their marriage license would provide their descendents with the date of the wedding, the names, ages, and occupations of the bride and groom, along with a host of other details about them on the day that they embarked on a new life together.*

young lovers may have eloped to a county where they were unknown, giving the clerk a false age, or ages, in order to procure their marriage license, making it difficult both to locate the license and to ascertain the couple's actual ages. Difficult, but not necessarily impossible, yet if your research proves fruitless and you are almost certain that a marriage did indeed take place (and keep an open mind about such family unions having been legitimized), it may simply be that the relevant documentation was never filed or has since been lost. Don't give up hope, however, because you may find evidence of the marriage within either religious records or the I.G.I. (see overleaf).

≈≈≈ *The certificate of the marriage of Mr G.M. Wilkins and Miss Emma Galtra in 1872 in Lane County, Oregon, is richly illustrated with symbols of love and marriage, along with a vigorous tree, a symbolic reference to the family that the newlyweds were expected to found. Has such a certificate been preserved by your family?*

≈ *Copies of English marriage certificates are always printed on green paper. The example at top certifies the marriage of John Westmoreland Gibson (whose middle name is spelled "Westmorland" in his son's birth certificate on page 66) to Charlotte Mamwell on September 9, 1858, in the parish church of the village of Grainthorpe, in the English county of Lincoln. The certificate below, which attests to the marriage of Robert Patterson and Maggie (Margaret) Kendrick on 29 September, 1885, at the Wandsworth Register Office in London, England, provides more useful details for the family-history researcher, notably the bride and groom's exact ages and addresses at the time of their marriage.*

DEATH CERTIFICATES

Roman Catholic memorial cards typically provide a wealth of biographical details about the deceased. The card that commemorates the life of Maria Schumacher, for example, specifies her maiden name (Rhein), along with the date of her death (June 4, 1917) and where she died (Bürrig, in Germany's Rhineland region). The text additionally details her date of birth (October 26, 1856), the date on which she married her husband, Peter Schumacher (January 28, 1882), and also notes that she was the mother of five children, one of whom predeceased her.

Although procuring an ancestor's death certificate may sound a morbid proposition, such a record may prove invaluable for a number of reasons. If your research is driven by the need to trace the course of a hereditary disease back through the generations, for example, such documentation may give you crucial information regarding the probable cause of a forebear's death. In addition, knowing where and when the individual died can pinpoint him or her, and thus also that person's immediate family, to a specific locality, while, if you are lucky, a death certificate may state the date and place of birth or, failing that, the age at which the person died, enabling you to calculate a probable birth date. You may also learn the name of the person (generally a relation) who notified the authorities of the individual's death, and, if the deceased was a U.S. resident who died after 1936, his or her Social Security number, thus opening up another avenue of research. Some records also give information regarding the date and location of the deceased's burial or cremation, while others may supply you with even more invaluable details in research terms, such as the deceased's parents' names and places of birth.

When searching for death certificates, follow the procedure outlined in the section on birth certificates. As previously noted, however, the date on which death registration was instituted, along with the information officially required, varies from country to country and, in the United States, from state to state, and how much useful data—if any—you are able to cull from a death certificate therefore depends on the recording policy of the authority in question at the time.

RELIGIOUS RECORDS AND THE INTERNATIONAL GENEALOGICAL INDEX

If your forebears were religious folk, there may be a wealth of information awaiting you in the records of the church, synagogue, or other religious community of which they were members. The primary importance of religious records to family-history researchers is that many predate the advent of civil registration in the nineteenth and twentieth centuries, so that if your ancestors were eighteenth-century churchgoers, for example, you may be able to add a welter of names, as well as dates and places, pertaining to christenings, marriages, and burials, to your list of forebears. And even if such information is already known to you, discovering additional evidence of such rites of passage can provide not only confirmation, but a host of extra details, such as the identity of the officiating priest, minister, or rabbi, along with that of any witnesses to the event.

If you already know that your ancestors attended a particular place of worship—and if they were rooted in one locality it is likely that family members would have remained loyal to it over the generations—it is worth contacting it to inquire if it holds any records that you could examine. Alternatively, and especially if you are unaware of your forebears' religious denomination, let alone where they worshipped, consulting the International Genealogical Index (I.G.I.) and other records gathered by the Church of Jesus Christ of Latter-day Saints (L.D.S.) can

Jesus! Maria! Josef! Stephanus!
„Wie es dem Herrn gefallen hat, so ist es geschehen, der Name des Herrn sei gebenedeit." Job. 1, 12.

✝

Betet für die Seelenruhe

der wohlachtbaren Frau

Maria Schumacher

geb. Rhein,

welche zu Bürrig am 4. Juni 1917, morgens 4 Uhr nach längerem, mit größter Geduld ertragenem Leiden, wiederholt gestärkt durch die Heilsmittel der röm.-kath. Kirche, sanft im Herrn entschlafen ist.

Die Verewigte war geboren am 26. Oktober 1856. Am 28. Januar 1882 vermählte sie sich mit Peter Schumacher, mit dem sie in überaus glücklicher Ehe lebte, die mit fünf Kindern gesegnet wurde, von denen eins der Mutter im Tode vorangegangen ist. Ihrem Gatten war sie stets eine fürsorgliche Gefährtin und

ihre Kinder erzog sie in wahrer Gottesfurcht zu treu katholischer Gesinnung, weshalb sie auch so sorgsam bemüht waren, der kranken Mutter in ihrem langen Leiden jede Erleichterung zu verschaffen. In ihrer Lebenszeit hat sie auch immer danach gestrebt, Gutes zu tun, wo sie nur konnte.

Regelmäßig ging sie zu den Sakramenten und war auch eifrigst darauf bedacht, daß sich ihre Kinder zu dem Empfang der hl. Kommunion einfanden.

Wir wollen hoffen, daß ihre liebe Seele bei Gott im Himmel ist. Sollte sie indessen wegen zeitlicher Sündenstrafen noch am Orte der Reinigung zurückgehalten werden, so empfehlen der hinterbliebene Gatte, die tiefbetrübten Kinder, die allzufrüh den Verlust ihrer so herzensguten Mutter zu beklagen haben, sowie die übrigen Anverwandten, dieselbe dem h. Opfer der Priester und dem frommen Gebete der Gläubigen, damit sie desto eher zur Anschauung Gottes gelange und

ruhe im ewigen Frieden.

Opladener Druckerei u.Verlagsanstalt

prove an illuminating first step. The I.G.I. is a vast database containing microfilmed transcripts of the records of a number of religious denominations, as well as some civil registrations of births, marriages, and deaths, dating from 1550 to 1920. The database is part of a program instituted by the L.D.S. to help its adherents to identify their ancestors so they can be retrospectively registered by living descendants as members of the church (which, according to Mormon belief, is an essential requirement if their souls are to be saved). Although the I.G.I. currently comprises 600 million names, with another 125 million contained within an addendum (figures that are constantly being added to as the L.D.S.'s agents continue the recording project all over the world), it is far from being a complete record. You may therefore fail to match your forebears to any of its entries. You should also remember that the laborious process of transcription prior to the advent of microfilm may have resulted in some inaccuracies.

Despite these caveats, the I.G.I. is an important research aid for family historians; it is also easy to access and use. Having entered an ancestor's name (the minimum requirement is an individual's first and family name, as well as his or her state or country of origin or settlement), you'll then be presented with a list of matching names and recorded events, usually baptisms and marriages (but not burials), along with the dates on which those events occurred and where. If, for instance, you homed in on a male forebear's name listed in association with a Church of England christening in the village of Grainthorpe, in the English county of Lincolnshire, in 1782, along with the day and month on which the infant was christened, you'll be presented with the baby's parents' names—in the case of married parents, the father's full name and the mother's first name. To ascertain the mother's maiden name, you should then enter the baby's father's name into the I.G.I. to see if it contains a record of his marriage, which should give you his wife's maiden name. If

your search is successful, you can then search for the christening records of both of the baby's parents, which should, in turn, give you their parents' names. Each entry is accompanied by information detailing its source, a baffling-looking list of batch and call numbers that it's vital to note down because these will refer you to the location of the original records should you wish to examine them in detail on microfilm or microfiche. Recording data sources is in any case an essential genealogical practice for the reasons described in Chapter 1.

If you have Internet access, launching yourself into the FamilySearch database that includes the I.G.I. couldn't be simpler: you'll find it at www.familysearch.org, where you can conduct as many searches as you want online at no cost. Linked to the I.G.I. within FamilySearch are two further databases maintained by the L.D.S: the Ancestral File database, which contains 35 million names, and the Pedigree Resource File, which includes details of 22 million individuals, while a further useful source available through the L.D.S. is the U.S. Social Security Death Index. In fact, the genealogical services and microfilmed archives offered by the L.D.S. are too numerous to describe in detail here, so take a look at its website for yourself. Alternatively, you could visit either the L.D.S.'s Family History Library Building in Salt Lake City, Utah, or else one of its three thousand offshoots, Family History Centers having been established in most U.S. states, as well as in many locations worldwide.

CENSUS RETURNS

Examining census returns is usually a highly rewarding exercise in that unlike birth, marriage, and death records, which typically only give the names of a few of the subjects' relations, each records family groups. The head of the household is named, along with details of those living in his or her home on the date designated as census day. The taking of censuses every ten years was instituted in 1790 in the United States, which means that your family's changing circumstances may theoretically have been recorded over the course of more than two hundred years. (The information gathered in such head counts in the United States was initially intended to ascertain proportional representation for the House of Representatives, but later also to provide vital-statistic data). Although national censuses were taken in England, Wales, Ireland, and Scotland from the early nineteenth century, many records were subsequently destroyed. Those available for England and Wales date from 1841; those for Scotland, also from 1841; and for Ireland, records are available from 1901.

You may not, however, be able to gain access to census records because not only are U.S. federal census returns from the past seventy-two years closed to public scrutiny (and in England and Wales the prohibited period is one hundred years) to protect the privacy of the living, but some of the pre-1850 returns have been lost due to administrative mishaps, while those of 1890 for the United States were largely destroyed by fire. Nevertheless, searching the available censuses may endow you with a series of snapshots of the past that together paint a vivid portrait of the highs and lows of your family's fortunes, as well as providing you with a treasure trove of genealogical details that it would have been impossible to glean from other sources.

Because the U.S. census program was—and remains—a federally run affair, the information given in census returns remains the same across the nation, whether your family lived in California or Connecticut, unlike vital-statistics records, which vary from state to state, depending on where they were registered. The format has not, however, remained the same over time. From 1790 to 1840, only civil districts and heads of households were named, for example, other family or household members simply being listed by color, age, gender, and status ("free" or "slave"). Supplementary questions augmented or replaced these within each successive census, so that by 1850 the name of every free household member was required,

as well as his or her age, gender, color, profession or trade (for males over fifteen), the value of any real estate owned, the state, territory, or country of birth, whether they had married or were in school within that year, whether they were unable to read or write (if they were over twenty), and whether they were "deaf & dumb, blind, insane, idiot, pauper or convict." Fast-forwarding over the decades, and cherry-picking some of the questions that may be of particular help to your research, the 1870 census asked whether each person's father and mother were "foreign-born"; the 1880 census, the first to require the household's mailing address, requested that each person's relationship to the head of the household be specified, along with their precise marital status and the birthplaces of their father and mother; while the 1890 and 1900 censuses included questions pertaining to immigrants (that of 1900, for instance, requesting the year of immigration, the number of years that the questionees had lived in the United States, whether they had become naturalized citizens, and whether they spoke English). Offering as they do such richness of detail, reading census returns will give you a fascinating—and sometimes heartrending—glimpse of your forebears' financial, marital, educational, occupational, and health circumstances, as well as numerous clues to lead your investigation in new directions.

The best way of making use of U.S. census returns as a tool for adding to your family records is to work your way back through time, starting with the 1920 or 1910 census. This advice is partly based on the likelihood that you'll have a rough idea which of your family members were alive in 1920, as well as their ages and relationship to each other. So, for instance, if you know your grandfather's full name, that he was ten years of age in 1920, and lived in a certain county in Iowa at that time, you'll have a better chance of finding a match than if you were searching the 1840 census for your great-great-grandfather, whose full name, date of birth, and place of residence you are unsure of. If you do find a match for your ten-year-old grandfather, and he was living in his parental household, you will be presented with his parents' names, ages, and places of birth, along with similar information for any of his siblings (because some may have died at an early age, but not before a census was taken, this is another way of establishing the existence of children whose vital records may otherwise prove elusive). This information will then enable you to target those census returns that will tell you, for example, where your grandfather's father lived, and with whom, at ten year intervals stretching right back to when he was himself a child. Working back through time in this manner can thus help you to build up a revealing picture of the ebb and flow of your family's fortunes and progeny, as well as give you helpful time frames and place names to aid your search for the vital records of any of the individuals listed in the census returns.

The key to unlocking the door to the data that may be awaiting you in the U.S. censuses takes the form of the census indexes, which catalog the census returns by state, county, community, township, precinct, ward, district, and so on. The first step in preparing to search the federal-census records is therefore to identify the state, and then the locality, in which you believe the family for whom you are looking was living at the time (for the censuses up to 1850, you'll also need the head of the family household's full name). The next step is to consult the indexes, which will direct you to the local-

ity's census pages. Entries for the 1790 census, and others, are held by many libraries, including Heritage Quest (the American Genealogical Lending Library), while those of 1800 through 1880 inclusive, along with those of 1900 to 1920, have been microfilmed by the National Archives in Washington, D.C., and these can be viewed either in Washington or at one of the offices of the National Archives Regional Archives System (see pages 98–99) or else rented through the National Archives Microfilm Rental Program (log on to the www.nara.gov website for further information). The L.D.S. Family History Centers also hold microfilms of U.S. censuses, along with certain English and Welsh population counts, while a further option is to go online and access the federal censuses at the www.Ancestry.com website (you will be required to pay a subscription fee before you can view them, however). In addition, note that censuses are increasingly being made available for loan or sale on CD-ROMs.

In order to locate your target families as speedily as possible using the indexes for the censuses of 1920, 1910, 1900, and 1880, you will need to familiarize yourself with the Soundex (also called Miracode) code, a one-letter, three-digit system into which family names are translated, which allocates numbers to groups of letters of the alphabet that sound phonetically similar, as in the chart below. Note that the five vowels, as well as the letters H, W, and Y, are ignored unless they are the first letter of a name. To find the Soundex equivalent of the family name for which you are searching, write down the name and then strike through any

ALPHABETICAL LETTER	SOUNDEX NUMBER
B, P, F, V	1
C, S, K, G, J, Q, X, Z	2
D, T	3
L	4
M, N	5
R	6

vowels, and, if they appear, the letters H, W, and Y, unless they begin the name. Now write down the first letter of the family name and then allocate a number to the first three letters that you are left with and write the numbers down. If two or more consecutive letters carry the same Soundex number, write down that number only once and replace the second, discarded number with the Soundex number relating to the fourth letter in line. If fewer than three letters remain, follow the letter(s) with zeros. If your family name is Hunt, for example, its Soundex code would be H530; Saunders would be S536; Kennedy would be K530; Henman would be H500; and Brenger would be B652. If the family name in question begins with Mc- or Mac-, perhaps McTaggart or MacAdams, ignore these prefixes and work out the Soundex code for Taggart or Adams, but if the name is preceded by Van, De, Le, or another European prefix, it is advisable to work out two Soundex codes, one including, and the other excluding, the prefix, and then to search for both Soundex codes in the indexes.

Once you have translated your family name into Soundex-speak, consult the state indexes to see if you can find any matching entries (abstracts of the full census return) for your Soundex code. If you do, one of these entries may list the family members for whom you are searching, along with the county in which they were living at that time, before finally directing you to the relevant enumeration district, sheet, and line number on which that family's census return appears. If you don't, consider the possibility of human error: maybe your family name was inadvertently skipped over when the Soundex index was being compiled, or perhaps the visiting enumerator misspelled the name, or was given a slightly different spelling, when the census information was gathered. (It was not for reasons of idle curiosity that questions about people's literacy and proficiency in English feature in many federal censuses!) In such cases, you may have to work through the census returns for the county or enumeration

district in which you believe your family lived page by page and line by line. Although it is always easier to search the census returns for sparsely populated rural districts than those for towns and cities teeming with people, tracking down your metropolitan forebears will be less headache-inducing if you know their addresses. Helpful aids include contemporary city directories (see pages 97–99), while the 1910 census is accompanied by street indexes for thirty-nine cities compiled by the Bureau of the Census.

Finally, should you hit the jackpot and find yourself staring at your family's census return, try not to become so overwhelmed by excitement that you forget to record such crucial source details as the identifying microfilm and roll number, along with the census page and line numbers, date, state and county, the number allocated to your family or their residence, and so on. However uninteresting this data may seem, it will instantly transport you to your family again should you need to revisit it: if you subsequently discover that one of your great-grandparents' sons had married shortly before census day, for example, you may want to peruse neighboring census entries to see if the newlyweds were living near his parental home. Also remember to transcribe the data given in the census entry exactly as it is written, even if you suspect that this information is not correct or consider it irrelevant. As you progress with the business of assembling the pieces of the puzzle, you may later find that it is indeed correct, or that the person listed as an orphan was actually an illegitimate offshoot of the family or that a boarder was, in fact, a visiting great-aunt who was offering a helping hand at a busy time for her family. And if you have the time, recording as many of the entries preceding and following that of your focus family often pays dividends, both in helping you to identify neighboring kinfolk and in building up a picture of the nature of the community in which your family lived. Family history is, after all, far more than simply a list of names and dates.

DOCUMENTATION SEARCH PLANNER

Person's Name and Number: ....

Document(s)/information to be located: ....
....
....
....

Sources for Research:	**Date Contacted**
Country, state, county, or city:	
Date or date range:	
Vital-statistics records archive:	....
Census records archive:	....
Genealogical society:	....
Local-history society:	....
Religious institution:	....
Occupational records:	....
Club or society affiliations:	....
Newspaper archive:	....
Period maps and photograph sources:	....
Ship's passenger records:	....
Property records:	....

Notes: ....
....
....
....
....
....
....
....
....
....
....
....
....

THE PAST IS A FOREIGN COUNTRY

If you are a citizen of the United States, it is likely that many of your ancestors would have been "foreign-born" individuals who spent much of their lives in far-off lands before making the momentous decision to begin afresh in the New World. There are many reasons why your forebears may have chosen to uproot themselves from their homelands, some of them life-threatening: they may have been desperate to escape religious, racial, or political persecution, for example, or else war, famine, or poverty. If you are of African American descent, some of your antecedents might have been transported to America against their will, their freedom being wrenched from them in exchange for the slavery imposed on them in the "land of the free." On a more positive note, not every immigrant who first set foot on alien soil did so under a dark cloud of adversity, heartbreak, or brutality, however, for many were propelled to distant shores by their robust spirit of adventure or their determination to seize the many chances for self-betterment—perhaps even gold—offered by a land of fresh opportunity. At some stage in your quest to discover more about your family history, you may therefore find that your trail comes to a halt, in which case the guidelines given in this chapter may enable you to pick it up again, but in another country.

When searching for immigrant or peripatetic ancestors, sticking to one of the golden rules of genealogy is especially indispensable: start with people whose vital details you know, and have proved to be correct, and then work your way systematically back through the generations, continuing to build on verified facts. Another general tip that is particularly pertinent when trying to identify any "foreign-born," Native American, or African antecedents (see pages 92 to 94 for more details on tracing Native American and African American forebears) is to keep your mind open to the possibility that the spelling of a family name may differ from the version with which you are familiar today. Because the attainment of a generally high standard of literacy across the populace and the standardization of spellings of proper names (both of which occurred only relatively recently) go hand in hand, expect to see many permutations in the way in which names are spelled, even such one-syllable names as Vere (Vear, Veare, Veer, and de Vere being just a few in this particular instance). In addition, remember that foreign-language family names were frequently Anglicized in America and Britain, so that a German family name, such as Schumacher, for example, may have been translated into its English equivalent (in this case Shoemaker), while the consonant-rich names of Poland were often adjusted to suit the English-attuned eye and tongue better, Jewish family names also frequently being translated or shortened to ease the social integration of their immigrant bearers as they strove to make new lives for themselves in their host country.

As well as immigrants, other wandering folk whom you may count among your ancestors include those who served in the military, whose absence from census records may be explained by the unsettled nature of their work, whether they were volunteers who'd signed up for the long term or more reluctant, short-term draftees. Also included in this chapter are pointers that will help you to discover more about any of your fighting forebears and the martial corps or theaters of war in which they served.

Wherever your ancestors originated from, and wherever they went during their lifetimes, most would have called some place

 With Britain's Houses of Parliament and Big Ben looming behind them, U.S. troops march across London's Westminster Bridge on September 5, 1917, bound for the battlefields of France. Many of these World War I combatants would not see their homes and loved ones in the United States again.

Passengers mill around one of Liverpool's landing stages. As Britain's primary Atlantic port, in the era predating air travel Liverpool was the usual point of departure for emigrants from England and Wales bound for the New World.

home, and for this reason the final section in this chapter introduces you to ways of learning more about any property—in its widest-ranging sense: land, businesses, money, and personal possessions—that your family members may have owned, property which, if they had once been dis-possessed, would have been doubly precious to them. And whether or not your forebears hailed from, or served in, another country, your own experiences as a time-traveler may give you a new insight into their lives and times, for, as the English writer L.P. Hartley observed in his novel *The Go-Between* (1953), "The past is a foreign country: they do things differently there."

IDENTIFYING IMMIGRANT ANCESTORS

Between the seventeenth and twentieth centuries, emigrants from Europe sailed across the Atlantic to settle in the New World in ever-increasing droves. It is estimated that those who arrived at New York's immigration center at Ellis Island (1892–1954) alone constitute the ancestors of around 40 percent of the current U.S. populace.

Your best chance of identifying an immi-grant ancestor, along with his or her coun-try of origin and date of emigration, lies in observing the general genealogical rule that the later the date you start with, the more

information you will uncover from documentary sources. Following this rule will point you in the direction of birth and death certificates (see pages 64 to 66 and page 70); census returns, such as the U.S. federal censuses of 1870 and later, which include increasingly detailed questions relating to foreign parentage, immigration, and the current status of any naturalization applications (note that in census returns "AL" represents an alien, "PA" denotes a declaration of intention having been filed, and "NA" signifies a naturalized citizen); and naturalization papers themselves, that is, the formal applications for citizenship of their host country made by resident aliens.

Taking the United States as an example, there are three categories of naturalization paper that your inquiries may bring to light: "first papers," or declarations of intention (to apply for citizenship), which were filed after the applicant had lived in the United States for two years; "final papers," which were filed three years later, comprising a petition for citizenship, an oath of allegiance, and proof of U.S. residency for the period of time (typically five years) specified as being necessary for qualification; and, finally, if the applicant was successful, certificates of naturalization. Such naturalization papers, which stretch back to 1790—the year in which the first naturalization law was enacted in the United States—are genealogically valuable for their insistence that petitioners state their date and place of birth, not just their country of origin, and sometimes also vital data relating to their husbands or wives and children, as well as the history of their immigration and subsequent residency in the United States.

Before 1906, naturalization papers could be filed at any U.S. court, but thereafter the requirement was changed to a federal court (but note that instances can still be found in state or county courts), which also issued certificates of naturalization. Begin your search for post-1906 documents by consulting the National Archives Regional Archives office (see pages 98–99) closest to the place where you believe your immigrant forebear or forebears settled. Another option is to write to the Immigration and Naturalization Service in Washington, DC (see page 97), for information and assistance in locating the relevant record. Alternatively, if you have reason to believe that a naturalization application was made before 1906, contact the relevant state archive to inquire whether it is housed there, and be prepared to have to trawl the records of local courthouses, too. And if your focus is on the Colonial era, note that the Library of Congress (see page 98), along with other historical archives, holds lists of the prospective colonists of foreign origin who were required to take oaths of allegiance to the British Crown prior to American Independence.

Another potentially fruitful avenue of inquiry leads to the lists of passengers aboard the ships that carried emigrants to major disembarkation centers, such as the American ports of Boston, New York, Philadelphia, Baltimore, and New Orleans or, in the case of many British emigrants, Australian and South African ports. In 1820, the U.S. government instituted a policy requiring ships' passenger lists to be filed at the customs house of the port of arrival, and by studying the customs' passenger lists maintained by the U.S. Customs Service you will typically glean the name of the ship that your ancestor may have traveled on, the name of its master, when it set sail, from which port it left, the one for which it was bound, and when it arrived there, along with the name, age, gender, occupation, and nationality of each of the passengers, although not their specific place of origin. Subsequent to the establishment of the Bureau of Immigration at New York's Ellis Island in 1892, which remained in operation until 1954, more detailed information was required from the huddled masses of hopeful immigrants for the completion of U.S. immigration passenger lists, such as their place of birth, their last permanent address, their intended final destination in the United

States (and, if this was a relative's residence, the degree of relationship, along with the relative's name and address), together with the names and addresses of their closest kinfolk in their former homeland. Infirmity, disability, and, from 1917, illiteracy disbarred emigrants from becoming immigrants, and records sometimes state the names of those unfortunates who were consequently deemed to offer little or no benefit to the U.S. economy and were therefore deported.

Those of the passenger lists that were originally filed with the U.S. Customs Service and the Bureau of Immigration and that have since been microfilmed can be viewed at the National Archives and its regional offices (see pages 98–99). The national archives of many European countries similarly often house collections of ships' passenger lists, so if you believe that your great-grandfather set sail from England to New York in 1900, for example, contact Britain's Public Record Office (P.R.O.) in Surrey (see page 100) to ascertain whether it holds the relevant record.

Although documentation relating to immigrants is relatively sparse prior to the nineteenth century, certain records do exist that may help you to trace forebears who left their homelands during the eighteenth century, and perhaps even the seventeenth. The P.R.O. in Britain, for instance, holds documents detailing the names, ages, occupations, and places of residence of English and Welsh natives who traveled to the American colonies to work as indentured servants, along with the names of the ships on which they were due to set sail, their dates of departure, and their intended destinations. Indexes to another useful collection of records (the papers themselves are archived at county courthouses) that may shed light on pre-Colonial ancestors can be found in the Library of Congress. Those who made successful applications to the British Crown, and later the colonial governing bodies, for land grants (see below) may have sent out a summons to people still living in their shared place of origin to work on their new estates—a potential source of clues.

RECORDS OF IMMIGRANTS/EMIGRANTS

NAME	DATE OF BIRTH	DATE OF IMMIGRATION	NAME OF SHIP	NOTES

TRACING MILITARY ANCESTORS

Before they left the peaceful rhythms of their day-to-day lives behind them to embark on military service, many enlisted men chose to be photographed in their pristine uniforms, often to give their loved ones a memento to cherish during their absence. Some men never returned, making such portraits, which must have been wept over time and time again, truly poignant family heirlooms. Apart from their sentimental significance, photographs of military men can provide you with useful clues: estimating the date of the photograph may enable you to match the man to the conflict that he was about to take part in, for example, while his uniform and, if they are discernible, his various insignia, may help you to identify his military unit. Armed with this information, you can then consult three of the most accessible categories of military records for family-history researchers: those chronicling wars fought both at home and abroad; those delineating the histories of specific regiments and other military corps; and those giving details of individual servicemen, notably militia musters, service and pensions records, and, in the United States, bounty land warrants.

While reading about the course of a particular military conflict can enhance your understanding of your military ancestor's wartime experiences, locating his service records will provide you with specific information about the private individual (what he looked like and his civil occupation, for example), along with evocative details of the highs and lows of his life as a military man from his point of enlistment to his date of discharge (and perhaps even beyond then if he qualified for a pension). The highs may highlight promotions and honors won in battle, while the lows may include being wounded, captured and imprisoned, or punished for a transgression against the military code.

If no photographs of military men—let alone any letters, or even medals, attesting to a forebear's military service—number among your family's collection of ancestral artifacts, and you have no anecdotal evidence hinting that any of your family members served in the military, certain other sources may alert you to the presence of a serviceman within your family tree. In the United States, for example, the federal census of 1910 inquired whether each person listed was a Civil War veteran, while that of 1840 requested the names and ages of any "Revolutionary or Military Service Pensioners in the foregoing [list of people recorded]." "A man who is good enough to shed his blood for his country is good enough to be given a square deal afterwards," as Theodore Roosevelt proclaimed in a speech delivered at Springfield, Illinois, on July 4, 1903, and ever since the United

A U.S. pilot of the 91st Aeronautical Squadron poses proudly in an airfield in France in February 1919. Even if you were uncertain of the photograph's date, the aircraft design and the style of the pilot's uniform would point you toward World War I or its immediate aftermath, while researching the pilot's insignia would reveal such further details as his rank and military affiliation.

 Josef Brenger's German Army passbook reveals that he was sworn in ten days before his eighteenth birthday in 1917 and that he survived the carnage of World War I, thereafter returning to the family farm in Düsseldorf-Eller.

☞☞ *During World War I, many governments recruited women into the military in behind-the-lines roles. Could a female ancestor of yours have been one of these patriotic Yeomanettes, pictured in June 1918, who enlisted in the U.S. Naval Reserve?*

the U.S.–Mexican War (1846–48), and the Spanish–American War (1898), as well as records relating to career soldiers and sailors, whether or not they saw action.

The indexes of many U.S. service and pensions records have been microfilmed and are widely distributed among research associations across the nation, but the documents themselves must be applied for by contacting the National Archives, which also holds a number of other documents generated by the military bureaucracy, such as bounty land warrants (detailing gifts of land made to military men who served between 1775 and 1855, applications for which include service details) and draft records. Note, however, that for reasons of privacy you will not be granted access to records under seventy-five years old. The National Personnel Records Center (see page 98), which maintains a selection of service records relating to the U.S. Army, Navy, Marine Corps, Coast Guard, and Air Force dating from 1864 to 1947, similarly restricts access to personnel documents to the named individuals themselves or their immediate relatives and descendants.

If your focus ancestor lived during the Colonial era, his name may appear among the militia (or, after the Civil War, National Guard) musters that were filed at town, county, and state level, making it worth contacting the relevant state archive for advice on tracking him down (and many such records are also preserved at the Library of Congress in Washington, DC). When requesting any type of military documentation, remember that you will at least need to provide your forebear's full name, roughly when he served, the state in which he enlisted, and, if you can, his unit, while if your search pertains to the Civil War, you must also specify whether your ancestor enrolled on the side of the Union or the Confederacy. Remember, too, that if any of your ancestors were immigrants, they may have served in the army of their country of origin, but be warned that documentary proof will certainly be more difficult to

States won its independence, taking care of the men who once took up arms in the service of their country has been government policy (as it is in other countries around the world, too). Military pension records can, in fact, provide you with reams of information, not only about veterans who had served in the military long enough to qualify for a pension, but also about those who, having been injured during the course of their service, were entitled to invalidity or disability payments, as well as about the widows or orphans of men who had died in action or who had inherited their husband's or father's long-term service pension. Existing alongside those of the Revolutionary War (1775–83) and Civil War (1861–65) are U.S. pensions records relating to the Indian Wars (dating from the 1780s to the 1890s), the War of 1812 (1812–15), locate—if it even exists—than if you are hunting for evidence of an American or British soldier's military career (British military documentation exists in abundance, and your first port of call when searching for information relating to a specific British soldier should be the Public Record Office).

A final tip is to enter the name of the conflict in which your forebear participated, or that of his unit, into an Internet search engine. Such is the explosion of interest in military history that the already impressive number of websites devoted to both the generalities and specifics of military life is growing almost by the day. One of these may help you to bring your quest to a successful conclusion, so if you try seeking for your military ancestor in this way, you may well find him.

MILITARY SERVICE RECORDS

NAME	UNIT	RANK	WAR(S) SERVED	CAREER NOTES

Perhaps your ancestors left the Belgian town of Tournai (above) after World War II, when the town sustained devastating bomb damage. Or perhaps they opened a general store in a gold-rush town like Dyea Point in the Yukon (near right), or opened an import/export store, like the one shown at far right, a Chinese goods store in Colorado.

PINPOINTING THE OWNERS OF PRIVATE PROPERTY

In his novel *Lord Jim* (1900), the English writer Joseph Conrad observed: "Each blade of grass has its spot on earth whence it draws its life, its strength; and so is man rooted to the land from which he draws his faith together with his life." These moving words are given additional poignancy through the knowledge that Conrad's family was rooted in Polish, not English, land, for it was not until he was twenty-nine that Teodor Jósef Konrad Korzeniowski became a naturalized British citizen. Having traded a storm-tossed life as a Polish seaman for an English gentleman's settled existence in the county of Kent, Conrad is buried in the Roman Catholic section of the city cemetery in Canterbury (ironically the official seat of the Church of England's primate). One of my own sets of great-grandparents rest there, too, my Irish-born great-grandmother, like Conrad and many other immigrants, having clung to the faith of her homeland as an anchor of constancy in an alien, albeit welcoming, land, a useful pointer that may help your search for immigrant ancestors.

Whatever your ancestral background—wealthy or humble, wandering or settled—human nature being what it is, most of your forebears would have aspired to root themselves in a place that they could call their own, and even if circumstances prevented them from achieving their dream of property ownership, they would probably at least have been able to amass a few moveable possessions (and perhaps some, having been passed down the generations, have today acquired the status of heirlooms within your family). Focusing on property records, notably land deeds, wills, and probate records, may therefore help you to discover more about the fortunes of your antecedents, as well as the things that they held dear, be it land, money that they had painstakingly saved, or material possessions that they cherished enough to deem them worthy of gifting to their loved ones in their wills.

In the United States, records of federal grants of public-domain land dating from around the start of the nineteenth century, together with details of bounty land warrants granted to military men (see above), private land claims, land patents, and the recipients of homestead farms after 1862, have been deposited with the National Archives, so if your focus is on one of these land records, contact either its headquarters in Washington, DC, or the appropriate regional office (see pages 98–99) for advice on discovering more. Alternatively, if you know that the land in question formed part of a specific county within a state-land state, contact the relevant county clerk's office to instigate a search of its land records, notably deed books, which typically include warranty and quitclaim deeds, deeds of gift and trust, and other types of legal document relating to the transfer of ownership of land or property, such as leases and mortgages. These may delineate in precise legal detail the location, character, and geographical features of a named tract of land, as well as

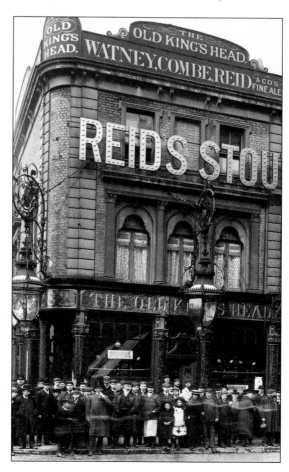

This London pub was demolished in 1906 to make way for a new road system. If your ancestors were forced to close or relocate businesses in similar circumstances, you should be able to locate documentation in a local archive providing full details.

the names of those associated with the property at that moment in time, and sometimes even earlier. When trying to match an ancestor's name to a piece of land, note that most deed books are indexed under the names of both the grantor, that is, the person granting or selling the land, and the grantee, to whom the legal ownership of the property was being sold or transferred. The Genealogical Society of the Church of Jesus Christ of Latter-day Saints has microfilmed many U.S. deed books, so a further option is to visit either one of its family history centers or its website (see page 97) for instructions on how to access these records. And if the land in question is in England, it's worth contacting the record office of the county of which it forms a part because many house remarkably detailed land records dating back for many centuries.

Wills, as well as their associated probate documents (probate being the process of officially proving a will to be authentic and legally valid), often give you a fascinating insight into the minutiae of a deceased per-

son's life, detailing as they usually do the names and addresses of witnesses, executors, and beneficiaries (in most cases kith or kin), as well as the value and description of the property bequeathed to the testator's heirs, such as real estate, patents, money, furniture, jewelry, and, before the abolition of slavery in the United States, slaves. Remember, however, that your ancestors may not have left a will, especially if they were female (before the twentieth century, married women in many countries, including the United States and Britain, were disbarred from making wills, although some made by property-owning spinsters and widows survive). You may nevertheless hit the jackpot if you initiate a search for an individual's will, the basic information that you will need being, of course, his or her full name, as well as when and where he or she died or was buried or cremated. In the United States, this data should enable you to target and contact the local county courthouse at which your forebear's probated will may have been filed (details of which were typically transcribed into indexed county will books between thirty and ninety days after the testator's death), along with an accompanying probate package containing all the legal paperwork that was required to validate the will.

In England and Wales, wills made after 1540 were required to be proved at one of the various courts established under the jurisdiction of the Church of England, that is, until 1858, when a switch to civil registration was made, whereafter wills were proved either at the appropriate district probate registry or at the Principal Probate Registry in London. Many probated wills predating the 1858 changeover have been microfilmed by the Church of Jesus Christ of Latter-day Saints, while indexes of those dating from 1858 can be searched at the Principal Probate Registry (see page 100, which also gives the address for postal applications for searches to be carried out covering a three-year period), from which copies of wills can be ordered for a fee.

Sturdza Palace in Romania, pictured before its demolition in 1938, around forty years after Dimitrie Sturdza commissioned its construction. Whether or not your ancestors boasted such a magnificent family seat, following the paper trail may lead you to uncover a wealth of details about the property that they owned, and to whom they bequeathed it.

RECORD OF FAMILY WILLS

NAME	DATE OF DEATH	WHERE DIED/BURIED	PROPERTY BEQUEATHED	TO WHOM

Fleshing Out the Bare Bones

This is a chapter of two distinct parts, focusing on the one hand on some specific problems that you may encounter on your family-history trail, but providing you with a wealth of ideas to help you to further your ancestral quest on the other.

The problems that are outlined, along with some suggested solutions, in the first part of this chapter are those associated with the various calendars that were used in times past; the difficulties inherent in searching for children who were born to unmarried parents or were given up for adoption; and the challenges posed when tracing one's descent from Native American and African American forebears.

The second part of this chapter includes general advice on how to tap into a mine of peripheral information by switching your focus to the records chronicling the history of your forebears' home locality. A host of contact details are given in the final chapter.

Solving Some Calendrical Conundrums

Along with all the potential confusion caused by the difference in U.S. and European systems of recording dates (that is, using month/day/year as opposed to day/month/year, see Chapter 2, page 57), you may encounter many further calendrical conundrums during the course of your family-history research, two of which are outlined in detail here.

The first is the replacement of the Julian (Old Style, or O.S.) calendar by the Gregorian (New Style, or N.S.) calendar—named for Pope Gregory XIII, who decreed its institution by papal bull—which was adopted by many European countries whose established religion was Roman Catholicism in 1582, and by various other European countries over the following years. It did not replace the Julian calendar in Scotland until January 1,

 Images of the past often resemble a foreign country: the citizens of Seattle, Washington, pictured going about their business in the Pioneer Square district in 1904, dressed very differently to those who tread the same streets today.

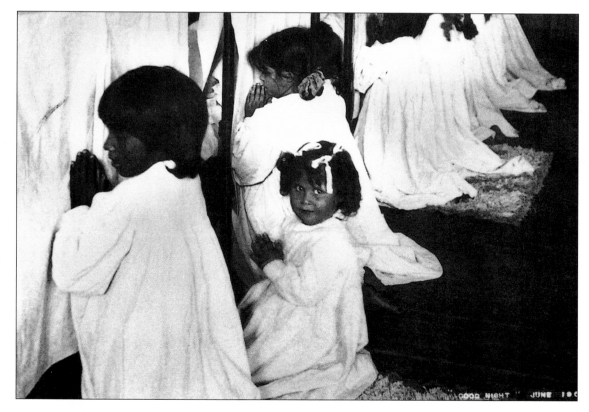

A small child appears delighted to be distracted from a prayer session by the photographer who visited Arizona's Phoenix Indian School in 1908. When researching Native American ancestry, tracking down school, church, and mission records can be a fruitful way of discovering more about elusive family members.

Urania, the muse of astrology in Greek mythology, is allegorically pictured in consultation with such luminaries of astronomy as Galileo and Copernicus. Numerous calendars have regulated life in the West over the millennia, sometimes as a result of astronomers' discoveries and sometimes for religious or simply political reasons.

1600, however, and it was not until January 1, 1752, that England, Wales, and the American colonies made the transition.

Under the Julian calendar, the first day of the new year was March 25 (Lady Day), March being deemed the first month of the year and February the last; by contrast, under the Gregorian calendar, New Year's Day became January 1, January being designated the first month of the year and December the last. If you find yourself recording any dates pertaining to England, Wales, and the American colonies from the eighteenth century, you should therefore bear the following points in mind:

- *the year of 1750 began on March 25, 1750, and ended on March 24, 1751;*
- *the year of 1751 began on March 25, 1751, and ended on December 31, 1751;*
- *the year of 1752 began on January 1, 1752, and ended on December 31, 1752, with September 2 being followed by September 14 (September 3, 4, 5, 6, 7, 8, 9, 10, 11, 12, and 13 being struck from the Gregorian calendar in this year only to bring it in line with the solar calendar);*
- *if you see a date written as August 1, 1732/33, the first year refers to the Old Style calendar and the second to its New Style successor (days of the month similarly often appear as double entries);*
- *if the number of the month, rather than the name, is given, note that, for example, the "first month" of 1738 is March, while the "first month" of 1780 is January.*

When recording dates from this era of calendrical confusion, it's best to follow them with the appropriate "O.S." or "N.S." abbreviation to clarify whether they relate to the Old Style or New Style calendar. (Note, too, that most Eastern Orthodox countries did not adopt the Gregorian calendar until the first quarter of the twentieth century.) Another point to be aware of is that many older documents specify the name of a saint's day or religious festival rather than a numerical date (Lady Day rather than March 25, for example), in which case refer to a calendar based on the appropriate religion.

If you have European ancestry, particularly French or French Canadian, the second problem that you may encounter is the French Republican calendar that was introduced to France in 1793 to signify the end of the *ancien régime* and the start of the new era of liberty, equality, and fraternity, which was used in France until popular dissent—and Napoleon Bonaparte—prompted their return to the Gregorian calendar in 1806. Nor was the French Republican calendar imposed on the French alone, but also on people living in the territories that were then under French occupation, such as the residents of the Rhineland

region of Germany. An example taken from my own collection of German vital-record documents issued in the civil-registration district of Köln (Cologne) illustrates the problem, in that it states that a male child was born on "*[le] vingtième jour du mois de Vendémiaire l'an douze de la République française*," that is, "the twentieth day of the month of Vendémiaire in the twelfth year of the French Republic." To determine the child's date of birth, you need to know that the French Republican calendar's retroactive starting date was also that of the French Republic, September 22, 1792. The twelfth year of the French Republic was therefore either 1803 or 1804, depending on the month, it having been decreed that each new year should start at midnight on the day preceding the observance of the autumnal equinox (which typically falls in September) in Paris. Consulting a list of names of the twelve months of the French Republican calendar will tell you that the Vendémiaire ("vintage month") was the first month, extending from September into October. It therefore appears that the child was born in October 1803, and consulting a conversion table of the days of the French Republican calendar pinpoints the day to October 13.

If you would like to gain a deeper understanding of these—and many other— calendrical conundrums, E.G. Richards's book *Mapping Time: The Calendar and its History* (Oxford University Press, Oxford, 1998) is highly recommended.

RESTORING STRAY CHILDREN TO THE FAMILY FOLD

Tracking down documentary evidence of a child born to unmarried parents can often prove problematic because it will usually not have been given its father's family name, so that if, for example, family lore insists that your great-great-great-grandfather, Thomas Kennedy, fathered a son out of wedlock, you may draw a blank when searching for a baby Kennedy in birth indexes. You will probably have better luck,

however, if you know the mother's family name, the prevalent convention in most countries having been to give illegitimate children their maternal family name. Note, however, that even if you locate such a birth certificate, the father's name may either have been invented by the mother, an acquaintance's name "borrowed," or she may simply have withheld it. There are, however, ways of filling in the blank space.

A German civil-registration document in my possession, for instance, indexed under the mother's family name, notes the birth, in 1828, of a son to a *Jungfer* ("spinster"), it being specified that she herself was the *eheliche Tochter* ("legitimate daughter") of her parents. Although the baby's father's name was not recorded, the names of two male witnesses to the registration present an initial clue to his identity. Details of the child's baptism (performed the day after his birth) in the records of a Roman Catholic church in the same locality reveal that the baby's male godparent shared the same family name as the first of the witnesses, suggesting that they were brothers. Finally, an addendum within the civil records confirms that the first male witness was indeed the father of the baby born to the *Jungfer*, also stating that the baby had been legitimized as a result of the subsequent marriage of his parents (a marriage certificate has not yet come to light, however, neither among the locality's civil records nor its church records, making the truth of this assertion dubious). As well as illustrating the differing types of data recorded in civil and religious documentation, this example shows how fruitful targeting the archives of a locality can be: as is often said, it's a small world, and people were less mobile and communities more tightly knit two hundred years ago than they are today.

A related issue is adoption. On reading a nineteenth-century census record, you may, for example, learn that a married couple in their seventies were sharing their home with a five-year-old girl who not only had the same family name, but was recorded as being the child of the householder (the husband).

This sets alarm bells ringing because it is improbable that the wife would have given birth in her sixties or seventies. Two primary alternative explanations present themselves: first, that the girl was the daughter of the husband by another woman, and, secondly, that she was actually the couple's grandchild. It you consider the latter alternative the most likely explanation, you'll need to get to work trying to discover which of the married couple's children was the parent of the child. In many cases, the solution can be found in the form of an unmarried daughter, who, because she was perhaps living and working elsewhere, or had died, was not listed as living in her parents' household on census day, and whose child may have been "adopted" by the grandparents. Indeed, it was common for close family members informally to adopt or foster orphaned or illegitimate children, and almost as common for hurried or overworked census enumerators to blur exact degrees of relationship.

Records of formal adoptions generally date from the twentieth century. In the United States, where adoption records are organized by state, many dating from the 1920s are sealed from public scrutiny, however. If you are searching for a twentieth-century English or Welsh adopted child, indexes to formal adoption records dating from January 1927 to April 1959 can be viewed at the Family Records Centre in London (see page 100), from which you can also order (for a fee) the records themselves. Among other details, these give the child's date of birth and adoptive name, along with the names and address of the parents who had adopted him or her.

Having a child out of wedlock was sadly such a social stigma in times past that people often went to elaborate lengths to kick over the traces (be particularly wary about taking such descriptions as "niece" at face value), so that deducing the probable birth parentage of an illegitimate or adopted child may require much detective work and poring-over of records. And when searching for the parents of any child born out of wedlock, be prepared for the possibility that although you may have your suspicions, you may never be able to confirm them with documentary proof.

LOCATING NATIVE AMERICAN ANCESTORS

If you've always been told that one of your facial features—perhaps the set of your eyes—is the legacy of a Native American great-great-grandmother, for example, and you'd like to discover more about how this mysterious individual may slot into your family-history puzzle, your quest will be difficult unless you at least know her name and, if not her tribe, roughly when and where she lived. From any local information you should be able to ascertain whether she hailed from a reservation or whether her family had become integrated into an ethnically mixed community, which, combined with her probable life dates, should then give you a promising location and time frame within which to search. Because the Native American tradition of recording history is largely oral, your best initial chance of tracking down any documentation that attests to her existence is to consult those archives whose records chart the coexistence of Native American peoples with more recent settlers. These may include some federal censuses, along with mission, church, court, or land records.

If the Native American forebear whose existence you are trying to verify belonged to one of the "Five Civilized Tribes" (Seminole, Creek, Cherokee, Chickasaw, and Choctaw) of the Southeast, your first step should be to consult the archives relating to the running of the Indian Territory, where the federal government obliged these tribes to settle during the nineteenth century. These can be viewed at both the National Archives in Washington, DC, and its Southwest Region branch at Fort Worth, Texas (see page 99), as well as at the archives of the Oklahoma Historical Society and the University of Oklahoma's Western History Collection.

If you are seeking an antecedent whose vital dates fall between 1830 and 1940, as well as the National Archives in Washington, DC, contact the Department of the Interior's Bureau of Indian Affairs (see page 98) to inquire whether it holds any records relating to your forebear's reservation (the tribal census rolls of 1884 to 1940, for instance, may prove particularly illuminating). It's also worth contacting as many of the libraries and historical societies in your ancestor's likely home state as you can to ask if they hold any data relating to local Native Americans: even if your ancestral name (see page 77, for some tips on researching ethnic names) does not feature within their books or records, you'll at least be able to gain a more detailed appreciation of the lifeways of your ancestor's community. Finally, because many Native Americans enlisted in the military, whether voluntarily or under duress, other potentially helpful sources may include military records (see pages 81 to 83).

IDENTIFYING AFRICAN AMERICAN ANCESTORS

"I was born in Tuckahoe, near Hillsborough, and about twelve miles from Easton, in Talbot county, Maryland. I have no accurate knowledge of my age, never having seen any authentic record containing it. By far the larger part of the slaves know as little of their ages as horses know of theirs. …I do not remember to have ever met a slave who could tell of his birthday. They seldom come nearer to it than planting-time, harvest-time, cherry-time, spring-time, or fall-time."
—Frederick Douglass,
Narrative of the Life of Frederick Douglass, 1845

Not only do the opening sentences of Frederick Douglass's autobiography starkly underline one of the many personal tragedies that beset the lives of most enslaved African Americans, but also one of the main difficulties of tracing African American descent: a lack of vital data. This problem is compounded by the further attempt to depersonalize those who were transported from Africa to America, as well as their enslaved descendants, by rebranding them with both Western first names and their masters' family names, so that someone who originally bore a name redolent of the rich history, culture, and traditions of Western Africa was forced to become an anonymous John Smith, for instance. Adding insult to injury for the family-history researcher, if early nineteenth-century federal censuses included a category for slaves or "free colored persons" at all, the enumerator was typically required simply to list their numbers, gender, and ages. The federal censuses of 1850 and 1860 (by which time the number of enslaved people was approaching 4 million) were expanded to request answers to such slave-related questions as "fugitives from the State" and "number manumitted [freed]," but because they required the names of the slave *owners* to be specified, only a slave's first name would be listed because it was presupposed that his or her second name would be the same as the owner's. To complicate matters further, many slaves cherished their original African family names in secrecy, sometimes over the course of several generations, only reverting to them openly when they became free. Others, after attaining freedom, would choose to be known by the family name of someone whom they respected, which would not necessarily have been their former "owner." Research becomes less frustrating following the abolition of slavery and the conclusion of the Civil War, when records at last begin to reflect African Americans' individual identities with the documentation of births, marriages, and deaths and detailed federal census returns.

Despite the difficulties inherent in tracing African American ancestors prior to the abolition of slavery, some sources may help you to track down relevant details, notably records relating to slave owners and the management of their estates, along with the archives of the Bureau of Refugees,

Freedmen, and Abandoned Lands (abbreviated to the Freedmen's Bureau), many of which you can view on their website, at www.freedmensbureau.com. Included in the former category are wills and property records (see pages 83 to 86), slaves, according to the preabolition mind-set, being their owners' property, held in the record offices of the relevant county, which may record the transfer of an African American maid's ownership from father to recently married daughter, for example, or the bequest of a father's estate, including the slaves who worked on it, to an eldest son in a will. The records of the Freedmen's Bureau, which date from 1865 to 1872, make more cheering reading, detailing as they do the myriad mundane steps that were taken to establish recently freed slaves in independent lives, as well as to bring former slaves from the same family together following their forcible separation through property transfers and to legalize marriages that had been contracted between slaves (unions that previously went unrecognized under U.S. law). You may discover another

potentially valuable source in the records of the Freedman's Savings and Trust Company dating from 1865 to 1874, which, in common with most—notoriously prudent—banks, contain a wealth of personal details about those who both applied for and received the benefits of its financial services.

If you can pinpoint an enslaved forebear to a specific locality, targeting the newspaper archives of the place in question (see below) may prove worthwhile because local newspapers often ran advertisements publicizing slave auctions or sales, as well as stories reporting the trial or punishment of slaves who were accused of committing a crime against their owners' person or property. Bear in mind, too, that your male African American forebears may have served in the military during the Civil War, and perhaps also in previous and subsequent conflicts, so if you suspect this to have been the case, contact the National Archives in Washington, DC, for guidance on locating the relevant records (it also holds nonmilitary records relating to African Americans, such as manumission and emancipation details, so inquire about these, too).

Finally, following two further trails may bring some previously elusive details relating to the life of an African American antecedent to light. The first is to examine the plantation records that are held by many local libraries and history societies, perhaps the most accessible of these being the Stampp collection (or, to give it its full title, "Records of Antebellum Southern Plantations from the Revolution Through the Civil War," compiled by Kenneth M. Stampp), microfilms of which have been widely distributed. The second is to surf the Internet, which is buzzing with contact details and information disseminated by both specialist organizations, such as Tulane University's Amistad Research Center (www.tulane.edu/~amistad/amfirst.htm), which is dedicated to the study of ethnic history, and individuals who are actively engaged in restoring the identities of enslaved African American people.

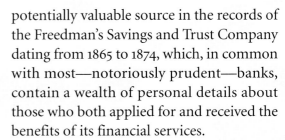

Following the Civil War and the abolition of slavery, African Americans were at last given the same legal rights, including the entitlement to purchase property, that their fellow U.S. citizens had long enjoyed. Some, like the Shores family (who shared their family name with their former "owner"), pictured here in Nebraska in 1887, opted to invest their time and labor in their own homestead.

BRINGING THE PAST TO LIFE

Learning more about the locality in which your forebears lived, such as its history, its geography, its economy, and the number and nature of its population, is vital if you are to gain a real understanding of your family history. Using a specific locality as a springboard, your leap into the past may prove a mesmerizing experience, for as you journey back through time, making brief stops along the way to sample the local color of a particular era, you'll find yourself becoming increasingly immersed in the day-to-day minutiae that formed the backdrop to your family's lives and times. If you have no luck in tracking down any documentation relating to a specific ancestor, but you know that he or she was a slave in Virginia in around 1830, for instance, a Seminole in the Indian Territory in 1880, an Italian immigrant living in Chicago in 1900, or a farmer in Ireland, studying the relevant contemporaneous records will at least give you an authentic taste of what that person's life would have been like.

If you are able to visit your target locality, or perhaps even live there, your initial port of call should be the local library, which will typically house all manner of publications, photographs, maps, and documents charting the history of the place, and whose staff may be able to direct you to further productive resources. Alternatively—or additionally—for the price of a small annual fee, you could join the local family-history society whose area of interest coincides with yours. Many local family-history societies publish quarterly journals that contain articles about the locality's history and populace, lists of all the family names (maybe including yours!) that its members are researching, and details of the publications and indexes to local records that are available to purchase. Joining the local-history society may also prove illuminating: not only do many also issue regular journals, but some have published the history of their local communities in pamphlet or book

form, often illustrated with period photographs, all of which will add local color to the picture that you are building up of your antecedents' lives and times.

A further way of adding vivid color to black-and-white place names is to examine as many historical and modern maps of your forebears' home locality as you can find, a strategy that will both bring their world to life—particularly if you can pinpoint their addresses—and provide an instructive lesson in the changing topography of the area. If your ancestors were citizens of a flourishing town or teeming city, another option is to look at city and town directories (and country settlements may be included within provincial directories), which, in a manner similar to telephone books, typically list the names of private citizens and businesses, sometimes by family name and sometimes by street (in what is called the householder's index), in alphabetical order. Again like telephone books, because such directories were regularly updated, sometimes even annually, if members of your family are listed within their pages, you may be able to ascertain whether their fortunes changed or they led relatively static lives. City and town directories can also act as invaluable guides to the makeup of census enumeration districts or wards, and if you know where your focus family members lived, but not where they paid their religious observances (if at all), scanning a directory for nearby places of worship will point you toward a potentially rich source of religious records detailing their rites of passage. As well as being held by local libraries, record offices, family-history and local-history societies, many U.S. and British town and city directories have been microfilmed and can today be viewed through the auspices of the Library of Congress and the Family History Library of the Church of Jesus Christ of Latter-day Saints (see pages 97 and 98), as well as other archives whose holdings transcend the local level.

There are few more evocative or detailed time-capsules available to help the family-history researcher than old editions of local newspapers, many of which have been transferred to microfilm or microfiche and can be viewed at local, county, state, or national archives. The national libraries of many countries also maintain newspaper-collection programs similar to that instituted by the United States Newspaper Program (visit www.neh.gov/preservation/usnp.html for further information about this program). If one of your family members was involved in a newsworthy event, such as an industrial accident or a military conflict, it is likely that his or her story would have featured in newsprint. In addition, if one of your antecedents was a prominent community member—a tradesperson, civic or political leader, athlete, entertainer, or pillar of society, for example—it is probable that he or she would have made frequent appearances within the local newspaper's pages. Just like today's newspapers, their predecessors in print also contain birth, marriage, and death notices, from which you may glean some vital missing details (and, in the case of obituaries, sometimes complete life stories leading you from the cradle to the grave), along with reports of crimes and punishments—perhaps a surprise is awaiting you!

If, however, your ancestral family name doesn't appear in old-fashioned newsprint, you will nevertheless learn a lot about the communal concerns of the locality, and through browsing through the advertisements of the era you'll also gain an insight into the types of goods, services, and events that your forebears were encouraged to buy, make use of, or attend. And if one of your ancestors owned a shop or business, you may even find an advertisement publicizing it. Further sources that may tell you more details of the working life of an antecedent who pursued a commercial or professional career are trade and occupational directories, in which you may find your target person's name, qualifications, the address of his or her business premises, as well as some examples of the goods or services that he or she offered, either as an individual professional or trader or as a company-owner or employee.

Only the main categories of historical documents relating to localities have been sketched in the suggestions outlined above; there are many more, and if you decide to investigate them further, you may find yourself striking genealogical gold.

☞ *Discovering a century-old postcard in your ancestral treasure chest may provide you with valuable information pertaining to a family member. The name of the addressee and the signature of the sender may reveal a family relationship, for example, thereby confirming an immigrant ancestor's country of origin, and perhaps even giving you a significant street name to research further, as specified on this postcard depicting the Rue du Bac in Suresnes, a suburb of Paris, France.*

SURESNES -- Rue du Bac et Place Henri IV   E.L.D.

Helpful Sources for Furthering Your Research

This section points you toward some of the thousands of websites, publications, and archives that may aid your research. (Note, however, that although these contact details are correct at the time of writing, changes may subsequently be made. Website addresses change frequently, so use a search engine in conjunction with the links below.) These sources will enable you to match some of the categories of genealogical documentation that are currently in the public domain with the organizations that hold them. Space restrictions inevitably limit the entries in this section, so we have concentrated on English-speaking countries. For resources in other countries, visit your local library to seek help if you do not have access to the Internet.

If you find that you've been bitten by the family-history bug, utilizing these resources may lead you further than you had ever envisaged, transporting you back in time as you learn about the lives of your antecedents.

Useful General Resources
The following are just a few comprehensive genealogical websites that also offer links to further online resources:

RootsWeb: *www.rootsweb.com*
The Genealogy Home Page: *www.genhomepage.com*
Cyndi's List: *www.CyndisList.com*

For the International Genealogical Index (I.G.I.) compiled by the Church of Jesus Christ of Latter-day Saints and other genealogical information, visit *www.familysearch.org*, contact a Family History Center near you, or write to:

Family History Department (L.D.S.)
Family History Library
35 North West Temple Street
Salt Lake City, UT 84150
Tel: (801) 240-2331

Resources for Tracing U.S. Ancestry
For guidance on locating vital records:

www.vitalrec.com

Two invaluable guides to locating vital records are: Kemp, T.J., *International Records Handbook*, Genealogical Publishing Co., Inc., Baltimore, latest edition; and Berko, R.L., and Sadler, S., *Where to Write for Vital Records of Births, Deaths, Marriages, and Divorces*, U.S. Department of Health and Human Services, Public Health Service, Hyattsville, latest edition.

For information on the federal censuses, contact:

Bureau of the Census
PO Box 1545
Jeffersonville, IN 47131
Tel: (812) 285-5314

For a subscription-only website giving you access to federal-census images for 1790 to 1910 inclusive, along with an index for the 1920 census, as well as parish and probate records for England, Wales, Scotland, and Ireland:

www.Ancestry.com

Aids for tracing the arrival of immigrant ancestors in the United States include: Filby, P.W., *Passenger and Immigration Lists Index: A Guide to Published Arrival Records of Passengers Who Came to the United States and Canada in the Seventeenth, Eighteenth, and Nineteenth Centuries*, Gale Research, Detroit, latest edition; and *Passenger and Immigration Lists Bibliography, 1538–1900*, Gale Research, Detroit, latest edition.

For information on viewing naturalization papers after 1906, write to:

The Immigration and Naturalization Service (I.N.S.)
U.S. Department of Justice
I.N.S. Historical Reference Library
    and Reading Room Section
Chester Arthur Building
425 I Street, NW
Room 1100A
Washington, DC 20536
Tel: (202) 514-2837

For information on obtaining records relating to military service, contact either the National Archives and Records Administration (see below) or:

National Personnel Records Center (N.P.R.C.)
General Services Administration
9700 Page Avenue
St. Louis, MO 63132

For further information on the history of U.S. military units, visit the U.S. Army Military History Institute's website at:

http://carlisle-www.army.mil/usamhi

For guidance on tracking down Native American ancestors, contact the National Archives and Records Administration (see below), as well as the Bureau of Indian Affairs at the following address:

Bureau of Indian Affairs, Department of the Interior
1849 C Street NW
Washington, DC 20240
Tel: (202) 343-1334

For information on the archives held by the Library of Congress, Washington, DC, visit *http://catalog.loc.gov;* and on those held by other libraries, *http://lcweb.loc.gov;* or contact:

Library of Congress
Local History and Genealogy Reading Room
Humanities and Social Sciences Division
Thomas Jefferson Building, Room LJ 20
10 First Street SE
Washington, DC 20540-5554
Tel: (202) 707-5537

For information on renting microfilmed genealogical material, contact by writing to or phoning:

Heritage Quest
P.O. Box 540670
North Salt Lake, UT 84054-0670
Tel: (800) 760-2455
www.heritagequest.com

American Genealogical Lending Library
P.O. Box 244
Bountiful, UT 84011

The National Archives Microfilm Rental Program
P.O. Box 30
Annapolis Junction, MD 20701-0030
Tel: (301) 604-3699
www.archives.gov

For information on archives, such as federal censuses, maintained by the U.S. National Archives, visit its website, *www.nara.gov,* or contact the following offices:

National Archives and Records Administration
700 Pennsylvania Avenue NW
Washington, DC 20408
Tel: (800) 234-8861 or (301) 713-6800

National Archives II
8601 Adelphi Road
College Park, MD 20740-6001
Tel: (800) 234-8861

For Alaska:

National Archives, Pacific Alaska Region (Anchorage)
654 W. Third Avenue
Anchorage, AK 99501-2145
Tel: (907) 271-2441

For Idaho, Oregon, and Washington:

National Archives, Pacific Alaska Region (Seattle)
6125 Sand Point Way NE
Seattle, WA 98115-7999
Tel: (206) 526-6501

For Arizona, southern California, and Clark County (Nevada):

National Archives, Pacific Region
24000 Avila Road
Laguna Niguel, CA 92677-3497
Tel: (949) 360-2641

For northern California, Nevada (apart from Clark County), Hawaii, American Samoa, and the Pacific Trust Territories:

National Archives, Park Sierra Region
1000 Commodore Drive
San Bruno, CA 94066-2350
Tel: (650) 876-9001

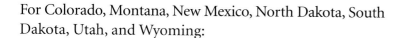

For Colorado, Montana, New Mexico, North Dakota, South Dakota, Utah, and Wyoming:

National Archives, Rocky Mountain Region
Building 48, Denver Federal Center
P.O. Box 25307
Denver, CO 80225-0307
Tel: (303) 236-0804

For the District of Columbia:

Washington National Records Center
4205 Suitland Road
Suitland, MD 20746

For Alabama, Florida, Georgia, Kentucky, Mississippi, North Carolina, South Carolina, and Tennessee:

National Archives, Southeast Region
1557 St. Joseph Avenue
East Point, GA 30344-2593
Tel: (404) 763-7474

For Illinois, Indiana, Michigan, Minnesota, Ohio, and Wisconsin (see also below):

National Archives, Great Lakes Region (Chicago)
7358 S. Pulaski Road
Chicago, IL 60629-5898
Tel: (773) 581-7816

For Indiana, Michigan, and Ohio:

National Archives, Great Lakes Region (Dayton)
3150 Springboro Road
Dayton, OH 45439-1883
Tel: (937) 225-2852

For Iowa, Kansas, Missouri, and Nebraska:

National Archives, Central Plains Region (Kansas City)
2312 E. Bannister Road
Kansas City, MO 64131
Tel: (816) 926-6920

For Connecticut, Maine, Massachusetts, New Hampshire, Rhode Island, and Vermont:

National Archives, Northeast Region (Boston)

Murphy Federal Center
380 Trapelo Road
Waltham, MA 02452-6399
Tel: (781) 647-8104

National Archives Northeast Region (Pittsfield)
10 Conte Drive
Pittsfield, MA 01201-8230
Tel: (413) 445-6885

For New Jersey, New York, Puerto Rico, and the U.S. Virgin Islands (see also below):

National Archives, Northeast Region (New York City)
201 Varick Street
New York, NY 10014-4811
Tel: (212) 337-1300

For various offices and courts in New Jersey, New York, Puerto Rico, the U.S. Virgin Islands, and the Department of Veterans Affairs:

National Archives, Central Plains Region (Lee's Summit)
200 Space Center Drive
Lee's Summit, MO 64064-1182
Tel: (816) 478-7089

For Delaware, Maryland, Pennsylvania, Virginia, and West Virginia:

National Archives, Mid Atlantic Region
(Center City Philadelphia)
900 Market Street
Philadelphia, PA 19107-4292
Tel: (215) 597-3000

National Archives, Mid Atlantic Region
(Northeast Philadelphia)
14700 Townsend Road
Philadelphia, PA 19154-1096
Tel: (215) 671-9027

For Arkansas, Louisiana, Oklahoma, and Texas:

National Archives, Southwest Region
501 W. Felix Street, Building 1
P.O. Box 6216
Fort Worth, TX 76115-0216
Tel: (817) 334-5515

RESEARCHING CANADIAN ANCESTRY

National Archives of Canada
395 Wellington Street
Ottawa, Ontario
K1A 0N3
Tel: (613) 995-5138

Canadian Federation of Genealogical
and Family History Societies
227 Parkville Bay
Winnipeg, MB
R2M 2J6

RESEARCHING BRITISH ANCESTRY

Useful guides for tracing British-based and Commonwealth ancestors include: Colwell, Stella, *Tracing Your Family History*, Hodder & Stoughton, London, 1997; Morris, Christine M., *Tracing Your Ancestors*, Salamander Books Ltd., London, 2001.

English and Welsh births, marriages, and death indexes, census returns, and some wills predating 1858, can be viewed at:

The Family Records Centre
1 Myddelton Street
Islington, London
EC1R 1UW
Tel: (020) 8392 5300
website: *www.familyrecords.gov.uk/frc.htm*

Written inquiries regarding postal applications for birth, marriage, and death certificates should be sent to:

Adoption/Overseas/Postal Applications Sections
Office for National Statistics, General Register Office
Smedley Hydro
Trafalgar Road
Southport, Merseyside
PR8 2HH
Tel: (0151) 471 4800

When searching for wills proved after 1858, write to or visit:

The Principal Probate Registry
First Avenue House
42–49 High Street
London
WC1V 6NP

For inquiries regarding postal applications for wills:

The Chief Clerk, Probate Subregistry
Duncombe Place
York
YO1 2EA

For further information on researching military ancestry and a host of other research categories:

The Public Record Office
Ruskin Avenue
Kew
Richmond, Surrey
TW9 4DU
Tel: (020) 8878 8905
website: *www.pro.gov.uk*

For information on a wide-ranging selection of genealogical services and resources, contact:

Society of Genealogists
14 Charterhouse Buildings
Goswell Road
London
EC1M 7BA
Tel: (020) 7251 8799
website: *www.cs.ncl.ac.uk/genuki/SoG*

For a list of local family-history societies in England and Wales, write to:

The Administrator, Federation of Family History Societies
The Benson Room, Birmingham and Midland Institute
Margaret Street
Birmingham
B3 3BS

For information on local-history societies, write to:

British Association of Local History (B.A.L.H.)
P.O. Box 1576
Salisbury, Wiltshire
SP1 8SY

For information on British newspapers, contact:

British Library Newspaper Library
Colindale Avenue
London
NW9 5HE

Tel: (020) 7412 7353
website: *www.bl.uk/collections*

For records in Scotland (birth, marriage, and death indexes from 1855 and census microfilms), contact:

General Register Office for Scotland, New Register House
Edinburgh
EH1 3YT
Tel: (0131) 334 0380
website: *www.gro-scotland.gov.uk*

For further genealogical assistance, contact:

Scottish Genealogy Society
Library and Family History Centre
15 Victoria Terrace
Edinburgh
EH1 2JL
Tel: (0131) 220 3677
Website: *www.scotsgenealogy.org*

The Scottish Association of Family History Societies
The Secretary
51/3 Mortonhall Road
Edinburgh
EH9 2HN
Tel: (0131) 667 0437

For Northern Ireland (birth, marriage, and death indexes for all of Ireland up to December 31, 1921, and for Northern Ireland thereafter):

General Register Office of Northern Ireland
Oxford House
49-55 Chichester Street
Belfast
BT1 4HL
Tel: (02890) 252 000
website: *www.nics.gov.uk*

RESEARCHING YOUR ANCESTORS IN IRELAND
Birth, marriage, and death indexes from 1864 are held at:

General Register Office
Joyce House
8-11 Lombard Street East
Dublin 2
Tel: (003531) 6711000

Irish censuses are held at:

National Archives of Ireland
Bishop Street
Dublin 8
Tel: (003531) 407 2300
website: *www.kst.dit.ie/nat-arch*

For further genealogical assistance, contact:

Irish Family History Society, The Secretary
P.O. Box 36
Naas, County Kildare

RESEARCHING AUSTRALIAN ANCESTRY
Archives Office of New South Wales
2 Globe Street
Sydney, NSW 2000

National Library of Australia
Parkes Place
Canberra, ACT 2600

Society of Australian Genealogists
Richmond Villa
120 Kent Street
Observatory Hill
Sydney, NSW 2000

RESEARCHING NEW ZEALAND ANCESTRY
National Archives of New Zealand
P.O. Box 6162
Te Aro
Wellington

New Zealand Society of Genealogists
P.O. Box 8795
Symonds Street
Auckland 1035

RESEARCHING SOUTH AFRICAN ANCESTRY
South African Government Archives Service
Union Building
Private Bag X236
Pretoria

Genealogical Society of South Africa
P.O. Box 2119
Houghton 2041

INDEX